Introducing Microsoft Teams

Understanding the New Chat-Based Workspace in Office 365

Balu N Ilag

Apress®

Introducing Microsoft Teams

Balu N Ilag
Tracy, California, USA

ISBN-13 (pbk): 978-1-4842-3566-9   ISBN-13 (electronic): 978-1-4842-3567-6
https://doi.org/10.1007/978-1-4842-3567-6

Library of Congress Control Number: 2018948206

Managing Director, Apress Media LLC: Welmoed Spahr
Acquisitions Editor: Smriti Srivastava
Development Editor: Matthew Moodie
Coordinating Editor: Divya Modi

Cover designed by eStudioCalamar

Cover image designed by Freepik (www.freepik.com)

Distributed to the book trade worldwide by Springer Science+Business Media New York, 233 Spring Street, 6th Floor, New York, NY 10013. Phone 1-800-SPRINGER, fax (201) 348-4505, e-mail orders-ny@springer-sbm.com, or visit www.springeronline.com. Apress Media, LLC is a California LLC and the sole member (owner) is Springer Science + Business Media Finance Inc (SSBM Finance Inc). SSBM Finance Inc is a **Delaware** corporation.

For information on translations, please e-mail rights@apress.com, or visit www.apress.com/rights-permissions.

Apress titles may be purchased in bulk for academic, corporate, or promotional use. eBook versions and licenses are also available for most titles. For more information, reference our Print and eBook Bulk Sales web page at www.apress.com/bulk-sales.

Any source code or other supplementary material referenced by the author in this book is available to readers on GitHub via the book's product page, located at www.apress.com/978-1-4842-3566-9. For more detailed information, please visit www.apress.com/source-code.

Printed on acid-free paper

This book is dedicated to my lovely wife and daughters Shravya and Chanda, who completed our family. And to the memory of my mother, Chandrabhaga, who inspired me with her dedication and simplicity. Thank you.

Table of Contents

About the Author

Balu N Ilag is a five-time Microsoft Most Valuable Professional who has MCSE: Communication and MCITP certifications. He works as a consultant and has more than 12 years of experience in Microsoft unified communications solutions including OCS, Lync, Skype for Business, and Microsoft Teams. He also writes an administrative blog on unified communications and has authored multiple administrative guides for the Microsoft TechNet Gallery.

About the Technical Reviewers

 **Vikas Sukhija** has more than a decade of IT infrastructure experience, and is certified in various Microsoft and related technologies. He has received a Microsoft Most Valuable Professional award three times in the Cloud and Data Center Management category (2015, 2016, and 2017).

With his experience in messaging and collaboration technologies, he has helped clients migrate from one messaging platform to another. He uses PowerShell to automate various monotonous tasks as well as to create self-service solutions for users. He has been recognized many times by clients for automations that resulted in direct and indirect cost savings.

He also has played a key role in helping large clients implement Microsoft Office 365.

Vikas can be reached through his blog (http://SysCloudPro.com) and Facebook (www.facebook.com/msexchange).

 **Prabhat** is 3 times Microsoft MVP, MBA, MCSE, worked as a Microsoft Architect for designing, implementing, managing and supporting solutions for private messaging cloud, mergers, collaboration between different messaging platforms and other migration & deployment projects for the following Technologies Office 365, Azure, AWS, Exchange, SQL, ADFS, MFA, FIM, MIM and Directory services. He currently works as CTO of Golden Five Consulting in Los Angeles USA.

He is also the CEO of LAEXUG Foundation. He blogs at MSExchange Guru.com. Prabhat also speaks at various conferences. He can be reached at prabhat.nigam@GoldenFive.net.

Acknowledgments

I want to thank the Microsoft MVP community and my friends for helping me to write this book.

Introduction

Microsoft Teams is a collaboration hub that brings conversations, persistent chat, calls, meetings, file content, and applications together in one place. *Introducing Microsoft Teams* gives IT administrators, consultants, and IT system administrators the comprehensive coverage they need to creatively utilize Microsoft Teams services.

Microsoft has added new capabilities from Skype for Business, SharePoint, and Office 365 groups to Teams. This book contains up-to-date information that walks you through industry best practices for enabling, configuring, integrating, managing, monitoring, and troubleshooting Teams with step-by-step instructions and examples.

This book has six chapters covering topics including Teams architecture, configuration, user provisioning and management, custom policy deployment, network requirements, the journey from Skype for Business to Microsoft Teams, and best practices. This book provides the answers you need and the insight that will make your job easier. This book's detailed coverage will help you exploit every capability that Microsoft Teams has to offer.

The author thoroughly introduces Microsoft Teams activation, provisioning, management, customization, access control, and use of all features. You'll find examples, details about challenges, as well as information about changes and improvements in Teams. This book has a chapter dedicated to troubleshooting that covers common troubleshooting scenarios.

Microsoft Teams is the only collaboration tool that has best-in-class features, and this book shed light on every feature—including conversations, activities, and meetings—that integrates with Office 365 and third-party applications. Organizations are looking to Microsoft Teams as a viable replacement for existing unified communication/collaboration tools, and Microsoft has already announced that it's adding new capabilities to Teams. Teams will evolve as the primary client for intelligent communications in Office 365, replacing the current Skype for Business client over time. Administrators need to be prepared for Teams intelligent communications. This book provides the step by step instructions you need toplan, deploy and use Microsoft Teams in your organization.

- Microsoft Teams Architecture

- Enable and configure Microsoft Teams

- Provisioning and Managing Users in Teams

- Teams capabilities and enhancement – Call and Meeting

- Administration of Teams and channels

- Manage and Control Teams using Custom Policies and PowerShell commands

- Managing Group access and Guest Access in Teams

- Teams Connectors and customization

- Implementing Quality of Service (QoS) for Teams

- Journey from Skype for Business to Microsoft Teams

- Overview of Microsoft Teams and Skype for Business Admin Center and other tools

- Microsoft Teams Troubleshooting

- Teams monitoring and Analytics

Author Balu Ilag is a support engineer, and his experience is reflected in the examples and step-by-step instructions he provides for each topic. These details will be useful for administrators, consultants, support engineers, help-desk users, and even end users.

CHAPTER 1

Introduction: Microsoft Teams

This chapter introduces Microsoft Teams as a collaboration tool. This chapter covers the following topics:

1. Microsoft Teams introduction

2. What Teams brings to organizations

3. License requirements for Teams

4. SharePoint, OneDrive, and Exchange interaction

5. Teams client availability and usage

6. Microsoft Teams architecture

7. Security and compliance

8. Authentication

Defining Microsoft Teams

Microsoft Teams is a collaboration tool that brings conversations, persistent chat, phone calls, meetings, file content, and applications together in one place. Users can use any device with enterprise-grade security, so they can confidently collaborate with others. Teams is nothing but an

© Balu N Ilag 2018
B.N. Ilag, *Introducing Microsoft Teams*, https://doi.org/10.1007/978-1-4842-3567-6_1

application that helps users pull together a team and collaborate using chat (conversation) instead of e-mails, and channels instead of just files and folders.

Teams has a workspace enabling users and their teams to securely edit their work files at the same time as well as see likes, @mentions, and replies with just a single click. Teams provides a platform that users and their teams can make their own by adding notes, linking to web sites, integrating applications, and customizing their experience in the cloud without location boundaries.

Microsoft Teams makes users more productive by giving them all the capabilities they require, including chat, audio/video calls, files and folders, meetings, and more.

Microsoft Teams leverages Azure Active Directory (Azure AD) to store identity information. Teams also integrates with other services within Office 365; for example, when you create a team in Teams, a SharePoint Online site and an Exchange Online group mailbox get created for each team.

The Teams persistent chat capability is provided by a chat service that interacts with the Office 365 substrate, presenting many of the built-in Office 365 capabilities, such as archiving and eDiscovery, for the data being exchanged in Teams.

Teams also provides a calling and meeting experience that is built on the next-generation cloud-based infrastructure also used by Skype and Skype for Business. These technology investments include Azure-based cloud services for media processing and signaling, H.264 video codecs, SILK and Opus audio codecs, network resiliency, telemetry, and quality diagnostics. This makes Microsoft Teams a unique application.

What Teams Brings to Your Organization

Nowadays, the number of users using online messaging, phone calls, calendars, and meetings has increased drastically. Microsoft Teams provides all of those services without compromising its application experience.

Using Teams, users not only can collaborate with internal team members but also can communicate with external team members through Guest Access outside their organization boundaries. Guest access is covered in Chapter 3.

Let's discuss in detail how users can use these capabilities.

Having Conversations and Chats

Microsoft Teams allows team members to communicate in real time and keep everyone updated at the same time. All team members can see and contribute to the team chat, and can check chat history at any time to recall past discussions and decisions.

Users have the flexibility to create private chats for small group conversations with one or many people, for those times when a conversation needs to be taken offline. They can stay on top of all of the chat activity with notifications that alert them when they are @mentioned or when someone replies to a conversation that they are a part of.

Users can also receive Skype for Business chat messages on Teams so that they have one place for their team communications.

This chat experience is supported on Windows, macOS, iOS, Android, Windows Phone, and on the Web—so there's no platform dependency for accessing Teams. Figure 1-1 shows a Teams chat.

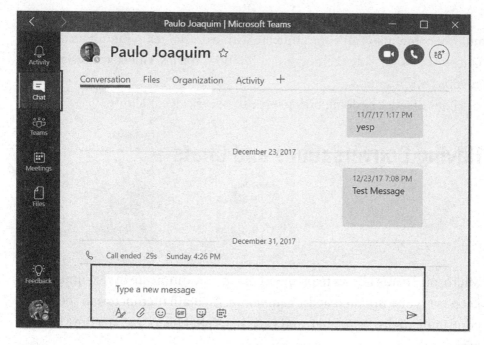

Figure 1-1. *Chat capability*

Using Teams Calls and Meetings

Microsoft Teams provides a great way to communicate within a team or outside Teams—not only through chats, but also through audio/video calls and meetings. Users can start a chat conversation and end up in an audio/video call. When users need to discuss something further, they can simply participate in a one-to-one or group call.

Teams provides great meeting experiences. An user can choose to meet now in an ad hoc meeting arising from a channel discussion, or can schedule a meeting by using Microsoft Outlook or Teams.

The experience of joining a meeting is seamless and of great quality.

To make a call via Teams, simply search for your contact and then click the Audio Call / Video Call option. Figure 1-2 shows a call being made in Teams.

Figure 1-2. *Making a call*

Using Teams for Teamwork

As I mentioned earlier, Teams is a true collaboration tool that provides users a single place where chat/conversations, meetings, calls, files, and everyday tools are available at their fingertips.

Users who want to talk face-to-face can start a video call from a team chat or a private chat. They can turn off video if they want just an audio call. They can also join scheduled meetings from Teams to meet within a channel or privately outside the channel. Figure 1-3 shows the chat options.

Figure 1-3. *Teams Audio / Video call options*

Because Teams is tightly integrated with Office 365, teams have quick access to the information that they need, whether they are using files shared through SharePoint, notes in OneNote, or tasks in Planner. Excel, PowerPoint, Word, PDFs, and other documents can be shared and opened right in the application. Figure 1-4 shows a OneNote note opened in Teams.

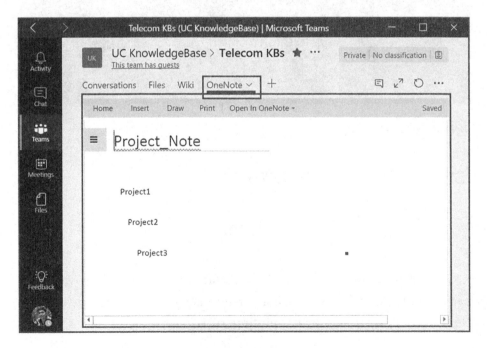

Figure 1-4. *Adding a OneNote note in Teams*

Users can search Teams for people, files, chats, and links; see Figure 1-5. They can switch easily between multiple teams. So, it's easy to see what's going on across teams, across channels, and across chats. Teams is also easy to set up and manage, whether the user is an IT professional or an end user. Because Teams is part of Office 365, all of that application's team members are instantly available as well.

Figure 1-5. *Search capability in Teams*

Currently, a team is limited to 999 people, including team members and the team owner.

Customizing Teams

Microsoft Teams gives you the flexibility to create a workspace that fits your team's needs. Users can create different channels for the team based on their work or needs. They can add new tabs to a channel for quick access to frequently used documents and cloud services such as PowerPoint and Planner. Teams also includes integrations from partners such as Zendesk, Asana, and Hootsuite.

Tabs are used to present content in its native format, allowing for rich collaboration in the right context. Figure 1-6 shows a tab added for a Word document.

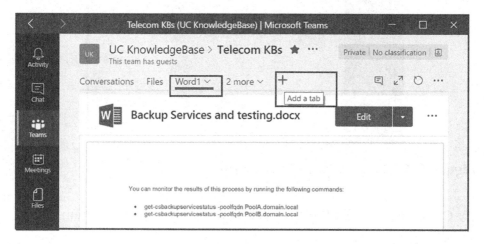

Figure 1-6. *Addding a tab for a Word document*

Currently, more than 96 Office 365 Connectors from services such as Twitter, Microsoft Dynamic CRM, Visual Studio Team Services (VSTS), and GitHub are available. Users can send rich notifications right into a channel. Notifications are useful for alerting a team about required actions, completed transactions, breaking news, and other real-time updates.

Users can use activity with notifications that alert them when they have been @mentioned or when someone has replied to a conversation they are a part of, as shown in Figure 1-7. Use @mention to get someone's attention in a channel conversation or a chat and @mention them.

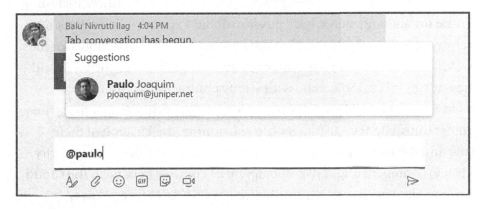

Figure 1-7. Sending an @mentioned notification

Keeping Everything Secure

As you know, Office 365 has strong commitments to security, compliance, privacy, and transparency. Teams was built using these same principles to deliver an enterprise-grade platform with enhanced security.

From the start, Teams was built with compliance, authentication, and privacy in mind. Teams has compliance built in, with support for industry standards including Grade B accessibility, ISO 27001 and 27018, SOC 1 and SOC 2, HIPAA, EU Model Clauses, and more.

Microsoft has added information-protection features that are useful for organizations: Archive, eDiscovery, Legal Hold, Compliance Content Search, Auditing, and Reporting. These features help organizations to control sensitive information if they have specific security requirements for content security and data use.

Teams protects team data by using strong security measures including two-factor authentication, hard passwords, and access policies. User data is always encrypted, whether that data is contained in chats, notes, or files.

Microsoft does not mine customer data for advertising purposes and does safeguard customer data with strong contractual commitments.

In keeping with Microsoft's commitment to providing customers the utmost transparency, customers can see uptime, the location of their data, and detailed reports of how Office 365 controls map to the security, privacy, compliance, and risk-management controls defined in the Cloud Security Alliance Cloud Controls Matrix, or CSA CCM (see `https://blogs.office.com/2016/02/03/how-to-assess-security-compliance-and-privacy-capabilities-in-office-365/`).

Teams is enterprise grade, with support in 31 languages across 181 markets and multiple data centers worldwide, a 99.9% financially backed service-level agreement (SLA), and 24/7 support.

License Requirements for Teams

Microsoft Teams is part of the Office 365 license suite.

To sign in to Teams, you need an Office 365 account with the appropriate Office 365 license plan assigned (for example, `bilag@mydomain.com` with an E3 license).

The following Office 365 license plans support Microsoft Teams:

- Business Essentials

- Business Premium

- Enterprise E1, E3, or E5

- Enterprise E4 (for anyone who purchased this plan prior to its retirement)

- Office 365 Education

- Office 365 Education Plus

- Office 365 Education E5, as well as existing Office 365 Education E3 customers who purchased E3 prior to its retirement

- Microsoft Teams isn't available for Government tenants yet.

Note   For Microsoft Teams calling, you must have E5 with a Calling Plan as an add-on, or E3 with an Add-on Cloud PBX and Calling Plan license.

IT administrators can easily turn on or turn off a Microsoft Teams license, as shown in Figure 1-8. By default, a Microsoft Teams license is enabled for users who have an Office 365 subscription plan license assigned.

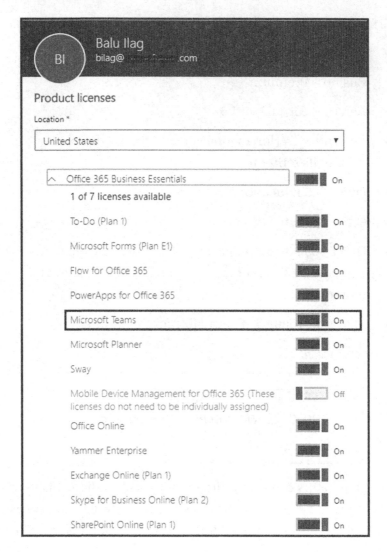

Figure 1-8. *Assigning a Teams license*

Microsoft recommends leaving the license enabled for all users.

If an organization is looking to pilot Teams, Microsoft recommends leaving the license on for all users, but notifying only the set of pilot users about the ability to leverage Teams.

IT administrators can use PowerShell to restrict the set of users for which you're enabling/disabling Teams licenses (see `https://technet.microsoft.com/library/dn771770.aspx`).

SharePoint, OneDrive, and Exchange Interaction

Microsoft Teams has multiple capabilities, and some features are dependent on Office 365 applications, such as Azure Active Directory, Exchange Online, SharePoint Online, and OneDrive for Business.

This section provides information on how Teams interacts with these services.

Azure Active Directory

Azure Active Directory is an important service that stores all identity information, including each user's user account and password. By using this information, users can sign in to Teams. As an example, a user account could be `bilag@mydomain.com`, and a password could be ABCDE123456.

Organizations that have an on-premises Active Directory can sync with Azure Active Directory to use single-identity authentication (a user account and password) to log in to Microsoft Teams. Microsoft Teams does support Modern Authentication.

Single Sign-on in Teams

The Microsoft Teams client supports single sign-on (SSO), which allows users to sign in to an app securely. If an user is logged into Windows through Azure Active Directory credentials, then the SSO process lets Microsoft Teams know that the user already entered their credentials elsewhere (for example, that user's work e-mail and password), and shouldn't be required to enter them again to launch the Teams app.

There are some dependencies for signing into Teams with Modern Authentication, including operating system/platform (Windows or a Mac). Dependancies will also vary depending on whether an organization has enabled single-factor authorization or multifactor authorization (multifactor authentication usually involves verifying credentials via phone, by providing a unique code or entering a PIN number, or presenting a thumbprint). Either way, after an user has completed the sign-in process by using Modern Authentication, that user won't be required to provide their credentials again. From that point on, Teams will sign into the account after the user launches the app from the same machine.

Exchange Online

Organizations must use Microsoft Exchange Online for an optimal Teams experience, because every time an user creates a team, a group mailbox is created on Exchange Online.

Every meeting created in Teams is pushed to the Exchange calendar. Then the Exchange calendar syncs with the Teams calendar to show all meetings on Teams so that user can see a single calendar experience.

Organizations that have Exchange on-premises can also use Teams. However, using Exchange on-premises has quite a few limitations; for example, the Teams client cannot create or view meetings unless users have Exchange 2016 CU3 and above, which means Teams integration with the calendar doesn't work with earlier Exchange versions. Also, users cannot modify the profile picture, cannot configure connectors, and aren't allowed compliance archiving of private chats without Exchange Online.

The Microsoft product group is working to allow earlier versions of Exchange on-premises to extend Microsoft Teams support. However, as of now, Teams support only Exchange 2016 CU3 and above.

SharePoint Online

Microsoft Teams uses SharePoint for storing files and folders. Every time an user uploads a file/document to a Teams channel, in the background that file gets uploaded to the SharePoint Online document library. So, every team is supplied a SharePoint site, and every team channel gets a dedicated folder where files are stored, and later these files are get shared in respective channel.

Currently, The organizations which are using SharePoint On-premises, they cannot use share file in the Microsoft Teams unless on-premises infrastructure is isolated. This behaviour may change in future.

OneDrive for Business

OneDrive for Business is used in Teams. Every time an user sends a file in a one-to-one chat or a private chat, that file gets uploaded in OneDrive. Specifically, the file is uploaded to the sender's OneDrive storage, and access permission is automatically set for the receiver so that they can then access the same data. For these functionalities, you must have SharePoint Online and a OneDrive license assigned.

To have the best experience and full functionality of Microsoft Teams, make sure of the following:

- All identities are present in the Azure Active Directory for Office 365.

- All mailboxes are homed in Exchange Online.

- All users are assigned and enabled with SharePoint licenses.

- All users are enabled for OneDrive for Business.

- Allow Microsoft Teams service URLs, IP addresses and port numbers on firewall or proxies.

- Most important, provide adequate training to end users.

15

Teams Client Availability and Usage

As shown in Figure 1-9, quite a few clients are available for Teams. These include the web client; desktop client (which includes Windows and Mac); and mobile apps for iOS devices, Android devices, and Windows Phone.

Figure 1-9. Teams client availability

Let's see more detailed information about each type of client.

Web Client

The Teams web client is fully supported with all the functionality of the Teams desktop client. At this point, real-time communications include scheduling and joining meetings, and making audio/video one-to-one and group calls in Web Preview.

To use Teams effectively, the browser must be configured to allow third-party cookies. No plug-in or download is required for the Teams web client.

When users browse the Teams site (`https://teams.microsoft.com`,) the web client performs a browser version check. If an unsupported browser version is detected, Teams will block access to the web interface and recommend that the user download the desktop client or mobile app.

The web client is supported by a variety of browsers. Here is a list of supported browser versions:

- Edge: 12+

- Internet Explorer: 11+

- Chrome: 51.0+

- Firefox: 47.0+

Note   Safari isn't yet supported in Teams, but it'll be supported soon.

As showed in Figure 1-10, Joining a web client meeting.

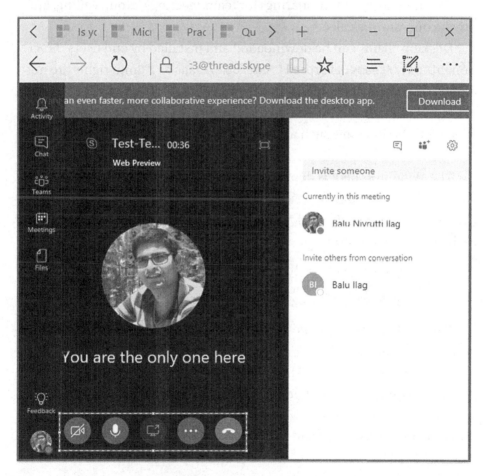

Figure 1-10. *Joining a web client meeting*

Desktop Client

The Teams desktop client is a stand-alone client that's available in both 32- and 64-bit versions for Windows. During installation, the client version will match the architecture of the Windows OS. At this point, the Teams desktop client is not part of the Office 365 ProPlus suite.

The Teams desktop client provides real-time communications support (audio, video, and content sharing) for team meetings, group calling, and private one-on-one calls.

Desktop clients can be downloaded and installed by end users directly from `https://teams.microsoft.com/downloads` as Admin rights are not required on Windows to install the Teams client.

IT admins can also download the installer and distribute it through client distribution tools such as System Center Configuration Manager (SCCM).

The Windows client is deployed to the `AppData` folder located in the user profile. Deploying to the user's local profile allows the client to be installed without requiring elevated rights. The Windows client is installed in the following locations:

- `%appdata%\local\Microsoft\Teams`

- `%appdata%\roaming\Microsoft\Teams`

For the desktop client, the Windows OS—specifically, Windows 7 and above—is supported.

When users initiate a call by using the Microsoft Teams desktop client for the first time, they might notice a warning about Windows firewall settings that asks for users to allow communication. Users can ignore this message, because the call will work even when the warning is dismissed.

Mac Client

To install Teams clients available for macOS, Admin rights are required on a Mac. The macOS client is installed to the /Applications folder.

For bulk client deployment, IT admins can use Casper Suite (macOS).

For the Teams Mac client, macOS 10.10 and above is supported.

Note   The Teams client updates automatically after initial installation; no update mechanisms are required.

Mobile Apps

Microsoft Teams mobile apps are available for Android, iOS, and Windows Phone. These apps are useful for users wanting to participate in chat-based conversations and allow peer-to-peer audio calls using their mobile devices.

To download Teams mobile apps, users can go to the relevant mobile store for Google Play, Apple App Store, or Microsoft Store for their mobile devices.

Teams mobile apps are distributed and updated through the respective mobile platform's app store only, and are not available to be distributed directly through mobile device management (MDM) solutions or side-loaded.

The following are the supported platforms for Teams mobile apps:

- Android: 4.4 or later

- iOS: 10.0 or later

- Windows Phone: Windows 10 Mobile

Managing Teams Client Updates

As I mentioned earlier, all the clients are currently updated automatically by the Microsoft Teams service, with no IT administrator intervention required. If an update is available, the client will automatically download the update, and when the application has idled for a period, the update process will start.

Microsoft Teams Architecture

Microsoft Teams is designed for the cloud, so it takes advantage of all new Office 365 features and applications that are available in the cloud, as they become available. Microsoft Teams is tightly integrated with various Microsoft applications in Office 365 and beyond.

Teams provides a chat-centric workspace that brings in a lot of Office 365 capabilities, including Office 365 Groups, SharePoint, Planner, Power BI, Office, Excel, Works, PowerPoint, Visual Studio Team Services, and bots. Partners can decide to build apps and bring them in to Teams.

Microsoft Teams is a hub side of services and Office 365 services and Skype Infrastructure are built on Azure.

Teams has a series of clients. These clients are not only built on the Teams API/layer but also are intelligent and powerful enough to talk directly to Office 365 services. Let's explore Microsoft Teams architecture next.

Teams Client Architecture

As mentioned earlier, we have a series of clients in Teams, including web and desktop (Windows and Mac) feature have shifted them on simultaneously. Teams also has mobile clients for iOS, Android, and Windows Phone.

As showed in Figure 1-11, Teams client architecture.

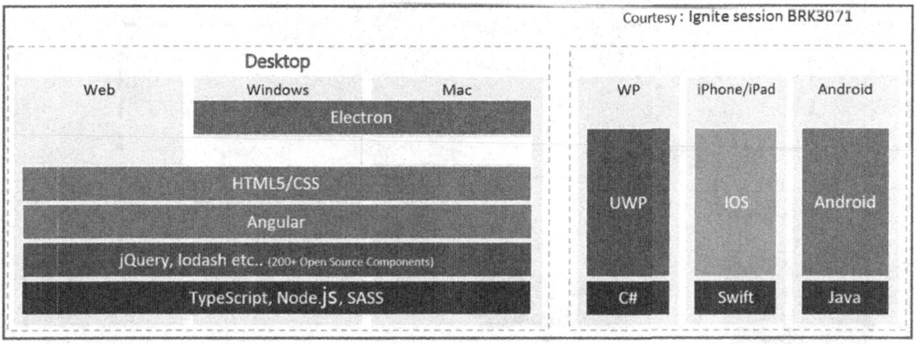

Figure 1-11. *Teams client architecture*

Each mobile app is native and built from the ground up, using a library that is necessary for talking to the Teams back end and other services' back ends.

The Teams desktop client architecture is the same as the web client architecture. The Teams client starts with TypeScript, Node.js, or SASS; and then jQuery, lodash, and so forth; Teams uses more than 200 open source components. The client is built up with the Angular framework and then standard HTML and CSS.

For the desktop client, Microsoft uses Electron and shell and then adds the native code for single sign-on and capabilities to have meetings, content sharing, and calling.

The users get same experience in using all these clients. All clients are automatically updated to use new Teams features.

Logical Architecture of Teams Conversations

Many components are involved in Teams conversations. Figure 1-12 illustrates this architecture.

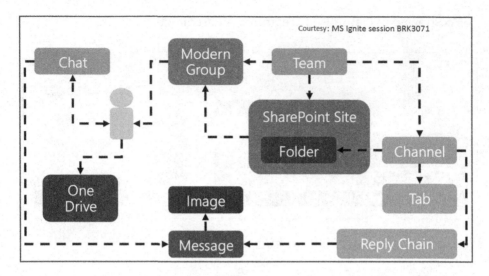

Figure 1-12. *The logical architecture of Teams conversations*

Multiple pieces talk to each other. This flow starts with the user having a conversation. That user is part of an Office 365 Modern Group that was provisioned for Teams. Every team has a Modern Group, every team has a SharePoint site, and every team has a set of channels where users can hold discussions. Each channel is mapped to a SharePoint site folder for file sharing.

Each channel also has tabs, which can be used to add Excel, PowerPoint, or Word documents to channels. Users can start meet now from same channels. Each channel has a reply chain that is used to keep track of replies. Each channel also has a set of messages, and those messages have images.

A user doesn't have to stick to only channels, but can initiate one-to-one chats, calls, and private chats. Users also can share files by using OneDrive.

Note   OneDrive is used for sharing files in a one-to-one conversation. SharePoint is used for sharing files in channels.

As showed in Figure 1-13, Teams services.

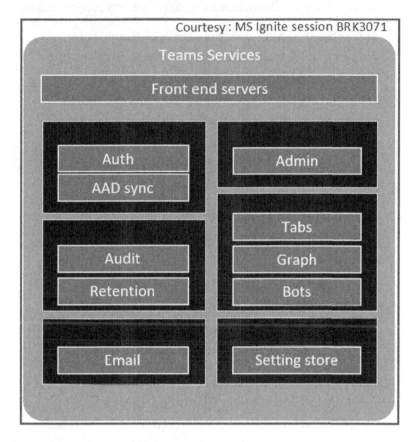

Figure 1-13. *Teams services*

Teams Services

Many services are used by Teams, and most of these services are orchestration components. Microsoft Teams communicates with Office 365 services for its capabilities. Microsoft Teams has front-end servers that allow to send HTML/JavaScript traffic payload and Enable Teams to handle configuration, getting the right version of the product with the right features turned on.

In the middle tier is a collection of microservices. Each service has a unique functionality that allows Teams to deploy each piece separately:

- *In Identity box*: Microsoft manages the Active Directory sync so that all Modern Groups stay in sync. Then authentication checks many things, such as whether Teams is turned on, whether an user has the Teams license assigned and turned on, whether an user has the rights to use Teams, and so forth. Authentication happens through mapping between AAD and Teams identity.

- *Compliance*: This is an important component; in compliance, there are two main services: Audit and Retention.

  - *Audit*: Any event will be audited that includes any request for Teams and other properties—for example, creating teams, adding members to a team, creating channels, and deleting teams or channels.

  - *Retention*: Most of the Teams chat data is saved to Office 365 mailboxes, Modern Group Mailboxes, and personal mailboxes for legal, eDiscovery, and other compliance purposes. Microsoft Teams will adapt retention configuration mention here but these configurations will over ride by application specific policies like information protection and Exchange online.

For example, if an organization decides to keep a one-month retention then, Microsoft has a service that purges that data from the rest of the system. There is connectivity between Office and chats.

- *Notification*: There is a firehose in chat services. If a user receives a message but is not online for 30–40 minutes, Teams will send an e-mail to the user's inbox. If a user has messages and replies that were missed, that also shows as part of notifications.

- *Team management*: Team management includes creating teams, creating SharePoint sites, and creating groups.

- *Extensibility*: There are many services including tabs, bots, and groups.

- *Configuration*: Metadata information is stored in a lot of places.

- For example, the chat service is stored in Skype and in groups. Other Teams-specific services are stored in Teams own metadata store.

Teams and Skype

Microsoft Teams is a chat-centric application, and its chat capabilities come from the rich Skype infrastructure, depicted in Figure 1-14.

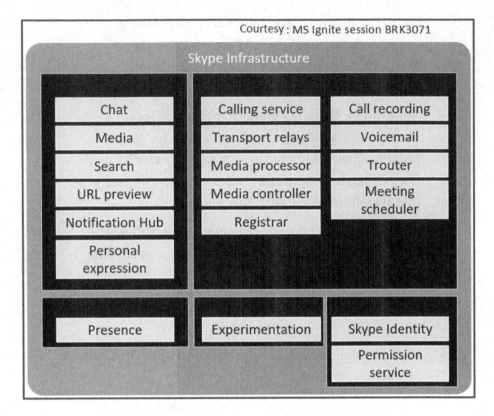

Figure 1-14. Teams and Skype

Teams has many chat capabilities, and all of these come from Skype. Let's discuss each feature:

- *Chat and media*: Here Teams stores images. All messages that are coming through can be searched, and you also can bookmark these messages to see later.

- *URL preview*: This service is like that of any modern app. If an user provides an URL, Teams will give a little preview of the web page.

- *Notification hub*: This will let you know when messages arrive in your client.

The media stack is already in common with Skype for Business Online. These components are used by both Teams and Skype:

- *Presence*: This is a status indicator; for example, Red/Yellow/Green shows user presence information.

- *Configuration experimentation*: Organizations can pick a set of users and enable them to use Teams to try a feature for testing.

- *Identity / Skype Identity*: A mapping exists between Active Directory users of Skype and Teams.

- *Permission service*: This allows access permissions, such as guest access for external users. This says it's fine for someone from outside Teams to contact other people in the tenant.

Teams and Office 365

Microsoft Office 365 is a platform for Teams, and Teams has tight integration with Office 365 applications. Many Office 365 cloud applications are used by Teams to give more capabilities to end users. These sets of applications are integrated and amplified in Teams, as shown in Figure 1-15.

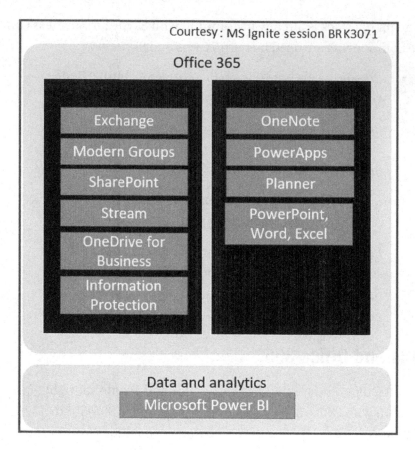

Figure 1-15. *Teams and Office 365*

The integrated applications are as follows:

- *Exchange*: Using Exchange, users can pull up calendar information and join meetings by clicking the Join Team Meeting URL in the calendar.

- *Modern Groups*: Groups play an important role in Teams. Every team has an associated group.

- *SharePoint*: SharePoint will be used to create SharePoint Team Site. As soon as an user creates a team, a SharePoint site for the team is created, and each channel has an associated folder.

- *OneDrive for Business*: This stores one-to-one shared data and files.

- *Information protection*: Information protection is provided by the Azure Rights Management service, and the same is used for Exchange, specific to Teams Information protection provided by Exchange, moving information data to the right place and getting the right signal back.

- *Application*: Users can use OneNote, PowerApps, Planner, PowerPoint, Word, Excel, and other applications in Teams.

- *Data and Analytics*: Teams has a call-quality dashboard for analyzing the call quality, plus Power BI and many other applications for building analytics.

Teams on Azure

Teams is basically built on Azure and uses Azure as a core platform. Azure has a massive scale and global footprint with redundancy.

Azure services include cloud services, storage, app services, media services, traffic manager, security center, Azure Active Directory, multifactor authentication, Azure Active Directory B2B, key vault, HockeyApp, application insights, event hubs, and notification hubs.

High-Level Architecture

As I mentioned earlier, Teams has many capabilities and integration with numerous applications. The architecture therefore includes multiple blocks that are interconnected. As shown in Figure 1-16, Teams clients are in the top tier, and Teams services are in the middle tier. This high-level architecture provides a complete overview of the way the various services work together to support Teams capabilities.

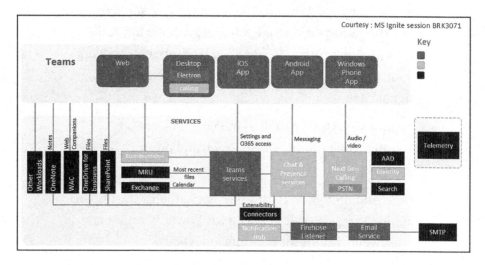

Figure 1-16. *Teams high-level architecture*

This is example on how Teams arch services together for providing functionality.

The Team process flow

When you log in to a Teams desktop client and authenticate through Azure AD, Teams gets information from the back-end store. Teams then creates a Modern Group and calls for a SharePoint site to be created. Teams then calls out to a chat service and uses the right object to handle teams, channels, and chats. Then it finally creates teams.

Chat Message Flow

To send a chat message, Teams clients talk directly to chat and presence services. The clients make a series of requests to sync data. Then chat request information notification data comes out. The client talks directly to the next generation via audio/video calls and PSTN (Public Switch Telephone Network).

As showed figure the notification hub, firehose listener, and e-mail services. So, chat and presence services talk to the firehose for any missed messages or missed @mentioned messages and then these get sent via e-mail notification.

Services are in the middle tier; for example, file access goes through the middle tier.

Security and Compliance

Microsoft Teams is built on the Office 365 cloud, which has advanced security and compliance capabilities. So Teams has security by design.

Teams information data is encrypted at rest and in transit. Microsoft Teams also supports Cloud Security Alliance compliance.

In the Microsoft compliance framework, Microsoft classifies Office 365 applications and services into four categories. Each category is defined by specific compliance commitments that must be met for an Office 365 service, or a related Microsoft service, to be listed in that category.

Service compliance categories C and D that have industry-leading compliance commitments are enabled by default; Teams is tier C–compliant. Which includes ISO 27001, ISO 27018, SSAE16 SOC 1 and SOC 2, HIPAA, and EU Model Clauses (EUMC).

Enabling Information Protection

Teams chat conversations are pushed to Exchange Online for information protection, as shown in Figure 1-17.

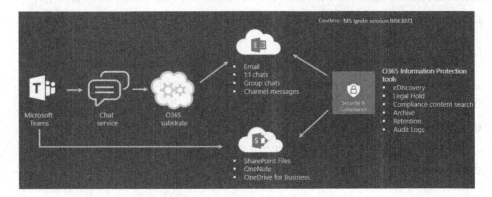

Figure 1-17. Information protection

Using Information Protection Flow

When user A sends a chat message to user B, the chat message goes to the chat services in the Teams back end. Then the message goes to the substrates, which will decide what to do with it. The chat is published to a hidden folder in each chat participant's mailbox as well as a group mailbox in Teams. If there is a file, it's stored in SharePoint, OneNote, and one-to-one file to OneDrive for Business.

Basically, Office 365 information protection tools including Security & Compliance talk to Exchange, SharePoint, OneNote, and OneDrive for Business to process that data for compliance purposes.

Teams also has support for audit log searches, eDiscovery, and legal holds for channels, chats, and files as well as mobile application management using Microsoft Intune.

Let's discuss in more detail how to use auditing/reporting, compliance content search, eDiscovery, and legal holds.

Auditing and Reporting

To use auditing, the IT administrator has to turn on auditing at the tenant level, which allows logs to be available. (It may take up to 24 hours after turning auditing on for the logs to appear.)

Log in to `https://portal.office.com`, and then select Security & Compliance Center. Click the Start Recording Now button, shown in Figure 1-18, to record user activity for auditing purposes.

Figure 1-18. *Enabling auditing and reporting*

Click the Turn On button, shown in Figure 1-19, to start recording user and admin activity to the Office 365 audit log.

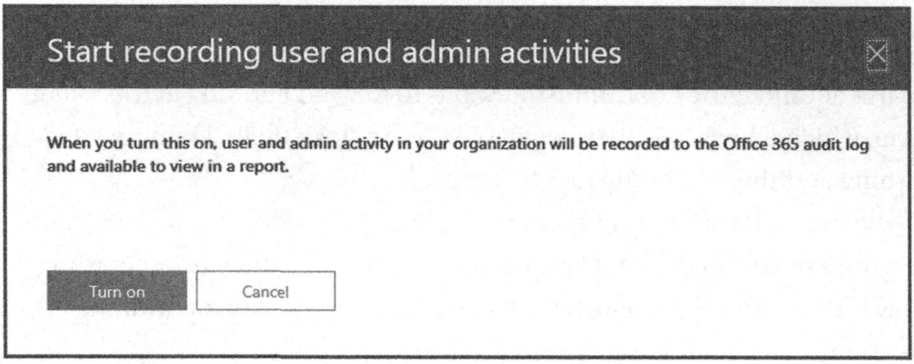

Start recording user and admin activities

When you turn this on, user and admin activity in your organization will be recorded to the Office 365 audit log and available to view in a report.

Turn on   Cancel

Figure 1-19. Start recording activity

Audit log searches are available through the Office 365 Security & Compliance Center, shown in Figure 1-20. This option allows you to set alerts and/or report on audit events by making available an export of workload-specific or generic event sets for IT admin use and investigation, across an unlimited auditing timeline. All audit log data is available for setting up alerts within the Office 365 Security & Compliance Center, as well as for filtering and export for further analysis.

The following events are captured when auditing is enabled:

- Creating a team

- Deleting a team

- Changing a team setting

- User signing in to Teams

- Adding members to a team

- Changing the role of members in a team

- Removing members from a team

- Adding a bot to a team

- Removing a bot from a team

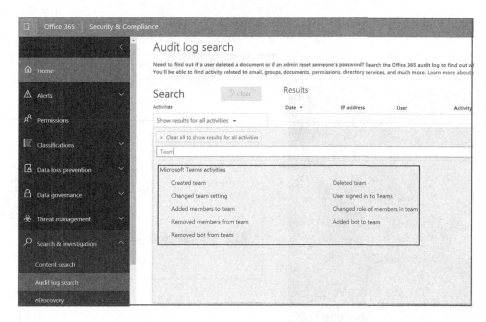

Figure 1-20. *Searching the audit log with various filters*

The complete event list across Office 365 is quite extensive and can be found at `https://support.office.com/en-us/article/Search-the-audit-log-in-the-Office-365-Security-Compliance-Center-0d4d0f35-390b-4518-800c-0c7cc95e946c?ui=en-US&rs-en-US&ad=US`.

Compliance Content Search

Teams has rich content search capabilities, which make searching faster through filtering; the search results are is exported to a specific container for compliance and litigation support. Compliance content search is available with or without an eDiscovery case. OneNote is covered only through content search.

As showed in Figure 1-21, Content search capability.

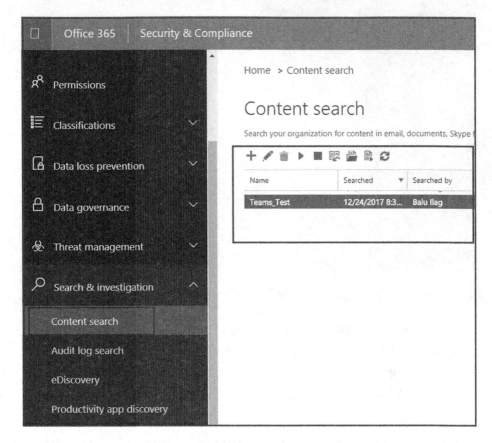

Figure 1-21. *Content search*

Content search and eDiscovery do not have to be enable within the Security & Compliance Center.

To learn more about how to leverage these services, see `https://docs.microsoft.com/en-us/MicrosoftTeams/content-search` and `https://docs.microsoft.com/en-us/MicrosoftTeams/ediscovery-investigation`.

eDiscovery in Teams

Electronic discovery (eDiscovery) is the process of identifying, collecting, and producing electronically stored information (ESI) in response to a request for production in a lawsuit or investigation.

Capabilities include case management, preservation, search, analysis and export of Teams data. This includes chat, messaging, and file data.

Microsoft Teams leverages Exchange mailboxes to store chat information. Any files uploaded in Teams conversations are covered under the eDiscovery functionality for SharePoint Online and OneDrive for Business.

Legal Hold

As I mentioned earlier, Teams has rich compliance capabilities. Legal hold is one of them. When any team within Microsoft Teams is put on In-Place Hold or Litigation Hold, the hold is placed on the group's mailbox. Legal holds are generally applied within the context of an eDiscovery case.

Authentication

Authentication is process of allowing an user to sign in to Teams and to use it. To sign in to Teams, the user should have an Azure Active Directory account and password. (For example, the account could be bilag@mydomain.com, and the password could be ABCD12345.)

Microsoft Teams supports more than one authentication option.

As I mentioned earlier, Teams is built on Office 365 and leverages the rich authentication options offered by the platform, including aligning with existing Office 365 Azure Active Directory authentication policies. Teams supports three authentication options, one of which can be used to sign in to Teams:

- Cloud identity

- Synchronized identity

- Federated identity

Cloud Identity

In this option, user accounts are located and managed in Office 365 and homed in Azure Active Directory. The account and password are verified by Azure Active Directory.

E.g. `Bilag@mydomain.com`

As showed in Figure 1-22, In Cloud identity account.

Figure 1-22. *In Cloud identity account*

Synchronized Identity

This authentication option is commonly used because a majority of organizations maintain user identities in on-premises Active Directory. In Cloud Identity account showed in Figure 1-22

Using this option, an user account is created and managed in on-premises Active Directory, but Teams is a cloud-based service. Therefore, these accounts and password hashes are synchronized to the cloud. In this method, users are entering the same on-premises credentials as they do in the cloud, while sign-in to Teams credentials is verified by Azure Active Directory.

The Microsoft Azure Active Directory Connect tool is used to synchronize credentials between on-premises Active Directory and Azure Active Directory. Authentication still occurs in the cloud.

As showed in Figure 1-23, synced user in Office 365.

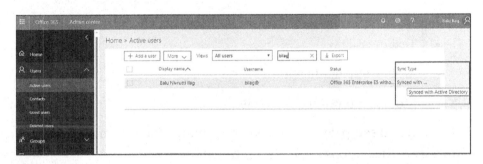

Figure 1-23. *Synced user in Office 365*

Federated Identity

Using the Federated Identity option requires a synchronized identity, with the user password verified by the on-premises Active Directory. With this model, the password hash does not need to be synchronized to Azure AD, and Active Directory Federation Services (AD FS) or a third-party identity provider is used to authenticate users against the on-premises Active Directory.

Federated Identity represents having an AD FS deployment; access to Office 365 services will redirect to the AD FS deployment for on-premises authentication and authorization.

Additionally, multifactor authentication (MFA), smart card, and certificate-based authentication are supported via Active Directory

Authentication Library (ADAL) integration. Depending on the authentication scheme selection, different MFA features are available.

Multifactor authentication is supported with any Office 365 plan that includes Microsoft Teams.

After users are enrolled for MFA, the next time an user signs in, they see a message that asks them to set up their second authentication factor.

Multiple options are available for multifactor authentication's second factor.

If an organization is using a cloud-only option, the following are available for the MFA second factor:

- Phone call

- Text message

- Mobile app notification

- Mobile app verification code

For a hybrid setup (Synchronized or Federated Identity model), the following are the options available for the MFA second factor:

- MFA for Office 365

- This will required Azure MFA on premises server is required to be deployed.

- Physical or virtual smart card (AD FS integrated)

For more information, refer to `https://docs.microsoft.com/en-us/MicrosoftTeams/identify-models-authentication`.

Signing in to Teams

To sign in to Teams, an user must have a sign-in address and password that has given by an IT administrator.

Simply download the Microsoft Teams client and open the Teams application. (Refer to the "Teams Client Availability and Usage" section earlier in this chapter.)

To sign in, type, for example, `bilag@mydomain.com`, as shown in Figure 1-24.

Figure 1-24. *Log in to Teams*

After you enter a password, you will be able to log in to Teams, as shown in Figure 1-25.

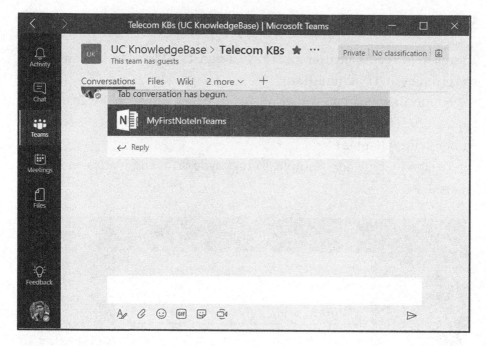

Figure 1-25. *Now logged on to Teams*

Summary

This chapter introduced you to Microsoft Teams. You learned about Teams benefits for you and your organization, various ways to use Teams, license requirements, available clients, services and core architecture, authentication methods, and compliance and security features.

CHAPTER 2

Optimizing the Teams Experience

In this chapter, you'll learn to enable and configure Teams with appropriate settings; you'll also deploy a Team client. This chapter covers the following topics:

1. Enabling and configuring Microsoft Teams

2. Creating teams

3. Preparing your organization for Teams

4. Enhancing productivity by using T-Bot

5. Deploying and updating the Teams client

Enabling and Configuring Microsoft Teams

When IT administrators set up an Office 365 tenant with an appropriate licensing plan, Microsoft Teams gets provisioned and enabled automatically, so there is no extra switch to enable Teams. However, multiple Teams settings can be turned on or off at the Office 365 tenant level. With Teams turned on for a tenant, any user that is also enabled for Teams will inherit the settings from the tenant level. To learn about Office 365 license plans and Microsoft Teams availability, refer to Chapter 1.

© Balu N Ilag 2018
B.N. Ilag, *Introducing Microsoft Teams*, https://doi.org/10.1007/978-1-4842-3567-6_2

So, all tenant settings get applied to all users.

If you have an Office 365 tenant, you are ready to configure Teams.

Note   Make sure you have Global Admin privileges before logging in to Office 365 to turn on the Teams experience.

Log in at the Microsoft portal (`https://portal.office.com`). Then click Admin to open the Office 365 Admin Center. Click the Settings option and then select Services & Add-ins, as shown in Figure 2-1.

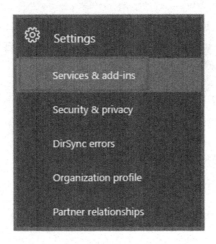

Figure 2-1. Office 365 services and add-ins

After the Services & Add-ins screen opens, search for *Microsoft Teams*, shown in Figure 2-2, and then double-click it.

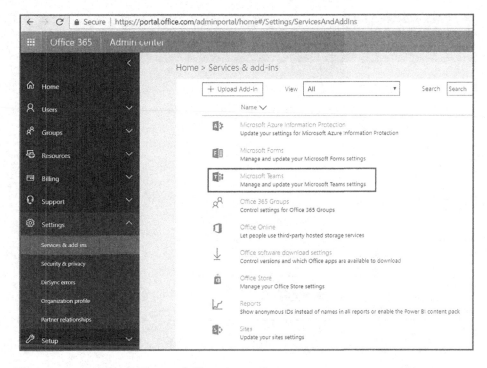

Figure 2-2. *The Microsoft Teams option*

As mentioned earlier, Teams is enabled by default at the tenant level. After the Microsoft Teams settings page is open, you will see Teams settings for the organization. Select the appropriate user/license type and then set its toggle to on (the toggle is labeled "Turn Microsoft Teams on or off for all users of this type"). Then click Save.

As an example, I have selected Business & Enterprise as the license type; see Figure 2-3.

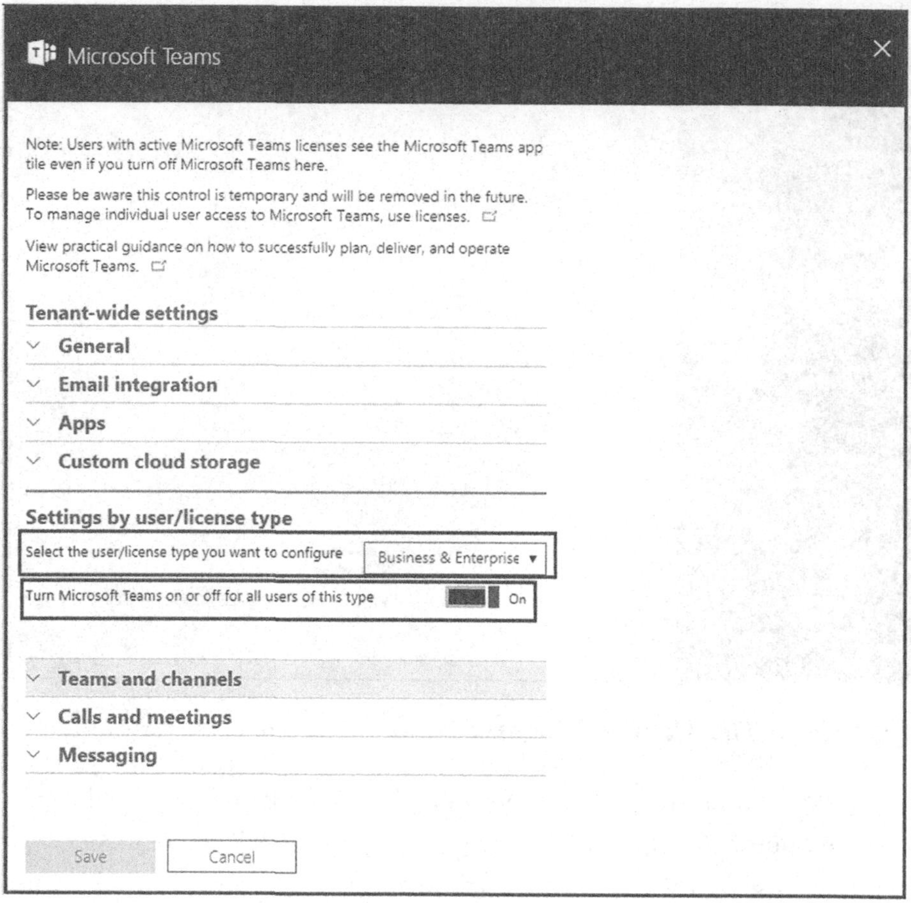

Figure 2-3. Enabling Teams for all users

Tenant-wide Settings

As you can see, multiple options and settings on the Microsoft Teams page are tenant-wide settings. These settings can be modified per your organization's needs. IT administrators can turn on or off these Teams organization settings under the Office 365 tenant.

Note   At this time, access to Teams will be controlled via user-level licensing only. There is no admin setting to turn off Teams for individual users.

General Settings

Under the General section, there are three settings, as shown in Figure 2-4.

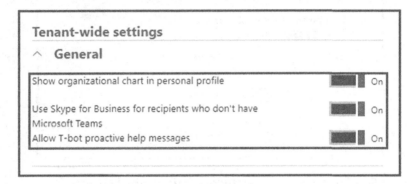

Figure 2-4.   *Tenant-wide general settings*

Show Organizational Chart in Personal Profile

A chart icon is under the user profile. This option displays a detailed organizational chart for the user. If this option is turned off, the chart will not display, as shown in Figure 2-5.

Figure 2-5. *Choosing to view the organizational chart*

When you click the View Organization option, the organizational chart will display, as shown in Figure 2-6.

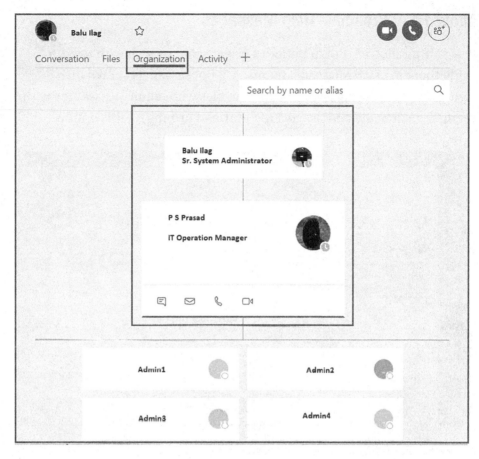

Figure 2-6. *Displaying the organizational chart*

Use Skype for Business for Recipients Who Don't Have Microsoft Teams

This is an important setting specific to interoperating with Skype for Business. Because organizations can have Microsoft Teams and Skype for Business together, they must be able to allow Microsoft Teams users to contact other users in the organization who are not enabled for Microsoft Teams via Skype for Business. I recommend enabling this setting to help users have a unified experience.

Allow T-Bot Proactive Help Messages

This setting allows T-Bot to initiate a private chat session with users to guide them in using Microsoft Teams. A T-Bot session is shown in Figure 2-7. This setting is helpful for newbies who require assistance with Teams functionality and usage. I recommend turning on this option.

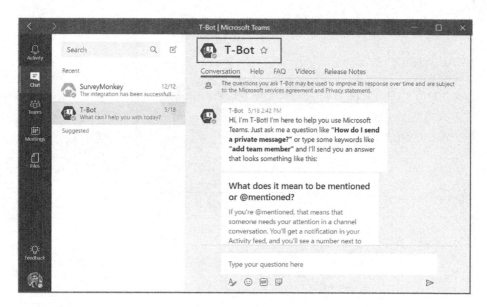

***Figure 2-7.** T-Bot help for Teams*

E-mail Integration

The E-mail Integration feature, shown in Figure 2-8, allows users to send an e-mail to a channel in Microsoft Teams by using the channel's e-mail address. Users can do this for any channel belonging to a team they own. Users can send e-mail to any channel. To enable an e-mail address for a channel, the user can select the More icon, which looks like an ellipsis (...), provided that user has permissions.

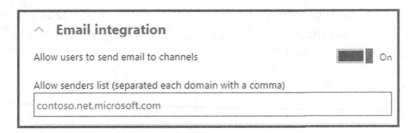

Figure 2-8. E-mail integration option

Allow Users to Send E-mail to Channels

This feature allows users to send an e-mail to a channel e-mail address that will get posted as messages. To find the channel's e-mail address, click More Options next to the channel name and then select Get E-mail Address.

Allow Senders List

This is a granular-level control for restriction of Simple Mail Transfer Protocol (SMTP) domains that are allowed to send e-mail to the Microsoft Teams channels.

Apps

As I mentioned earlier, Teams allows seamless application integration. Apps in Microsoft Teams are the best way to integrate the tools and services in Teams. After enabling apps, in Teams administrators can select which application they want to be available for Teams in their organization.

The Apps section, shown in Figure 2-9, lets you configure the following settings for your organization:

- *Allow external apps in Microsoft Teams*: This setting allows users to access all external applications from

Teams. When this option is enabled, users can add tabs
and bots (here *bot* indicates a different bot than T-Bot)
that are available to the Office 365 tenant.

- *Allow sideloading of external apps*: This setting allows
  users to install and enable custom bots and tabs in
  their Teams.

- *Enable new external apps by default*: This option
  enables external apps in Teams, as shown in Figure 2-9.

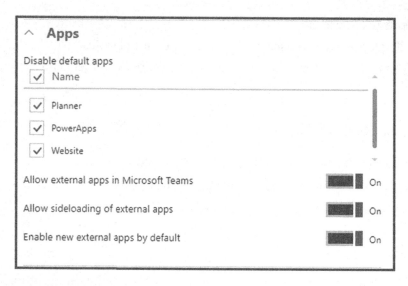

Figure 2-9. *Enabling apps in Teams*

Custom Cloud Storage

Cloud storage options in Microsoft Teams currently include Box, Dropbox,
Google Drive, and ShareFile. Users can upload and share files from cloud
storage services in Microsoft Teams, channels, and chats.

IT administrators can control this option by clicking the toggle switch next to the cloud storage providers that your organization wants to use, as shown in Figure 2-10.

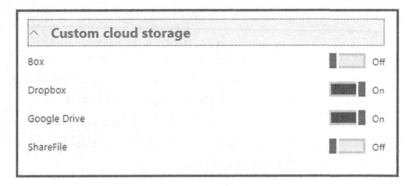

Figure 2-10. *Cloud storage*

Settings by User/License Type

In the user settings by license, IT administrators can turn on or turn off options in Teams and channels, calls and meetings, and messaging. You can see these options in Figure 2-11.

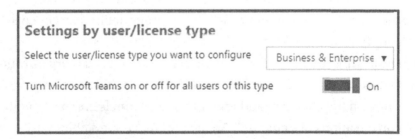

Figure 2-11. *User/license type*

Teams and Channels

As mentioned earlier, Microsoft Teams is built to provide collaboration capabilities to people. Teams is designed to bring together a group of people who work closely to get things done and work toward achieving a similar goal.

Teams provides multiple capabilities, and IT administrators can control these capabilities. For example, IT administrators can manage team owners and members by using the Groups dashboard in the Office 365 Admin Center portal. In the Teams and Channels section, shown in Figure 2-12, click the link for "Use the Groups dashboard in the Office 365 admin center to manage teams."

> ⌃ **Teams and channels**
>
> Use the Groups dashboard in admin center to manage teams. ☐
>
> Anyone on the team can add and manage channels. ☐

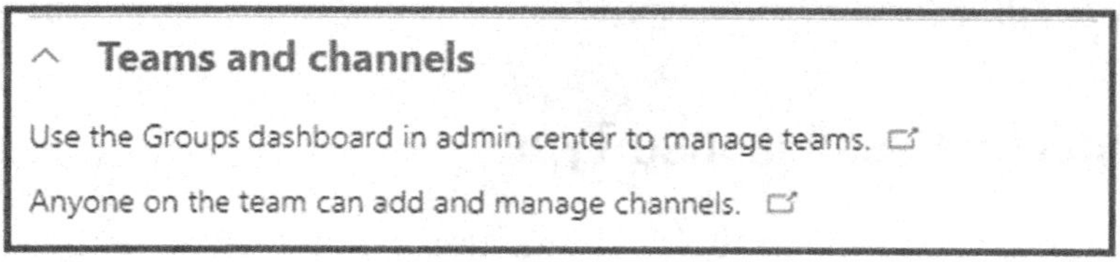

Figure 2-12. *Settings for teams and channels*

IT administrators can control which users in your organization can create teams in Teams. The same creation settings defined by Office 365 groups apply to Teams.

Channels are subcategories of teams. For example, if IT Organization is a team, then Telecom, Infrastructure, and Storage could be the channels.

Anyone on the team can add and manage channels and participate in the conversations in a channel. An user might create a channel for an activity or for a department. Conversations, files, and wikis are specific to each channel, but all members of the team can see them.

Calls and Meetings

Teams provides great ways to collaborate, including chat, audio/video calls, scheduled and ad hoc meetings, desktop sharing, and more. The Calls and Meetings section, shown in Figure 2-13, provides options for configuring the various collaboration settings for your organization. This section also allows you to control calling, meeting, and screen-sharing features using Teams in your organization.

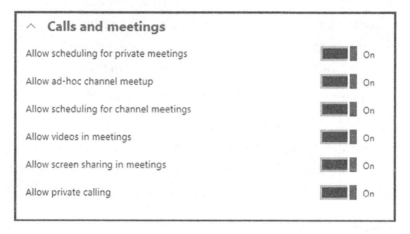

Figure 2-13. Calls and meetings

Options in the Calls and Meetings section are as follows:

- *Allow scheduling for private meetings*: Allows users to schedule private meetings that are not listed in any channel.

- *Allow ad hoc channel meetup*: Allows users to have ad hoc meetings while a conversation is in progress on the channel; conversation participants can easily join with a single click. An ad hoc meeting is also known as *Meet Now*.

- *Allow scheduling for channel meetings*: Allows users to schedule a meeting for a channel that all channel members can easily join with a single click.

- *Allow videos in meetings*: After enabling this option, users can use video in meetings. I recommend turning on this option, because using audio/video in meetings is a great way for participants to express their viewpoints.

- *Allow screen sharing in meetings*: Screen sharing is another great modality to use in meetings. By allowing this option, users can use screen sharing in meetings.

- *Allow private calling*: When this option is enabled, users can make private calls.

The maximum number of people in a meeting is 80. There can be 20 members in a private chat, including the user who created the chat conversation.

Messaging

Messaging is another important section. Multiple settings can be configured under the Messaging section, as shown in Figure 2-14.

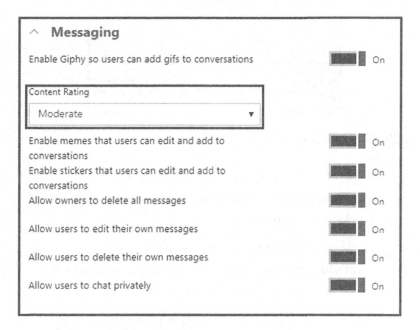

Figure 2-14. *Messaging options*

The options in the Messaging section are as follows:

- *Enable Giphy so users can add gifs to conversations*: Allows users to use animated pictures within the conversations.

- *Content Rating*: When animated images are turned on, content ratings can be applied to restrict the type of animated images that can be displayed in conversations. Available content rating options, shown in Figure 2-15, are as follows:

    - Strict

    - Moderate (the default value)

    - Allow all content

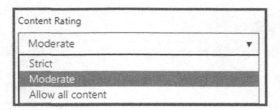

Figure 2-15. *Content ratings*

- *Enable memes that users can edit and add to conversations*: Allows users to use Internet memes to make humorous posts.

- *Enable stickers that users can edit and add to conversations*: Allows users to post images with editable text to get channel members' attention.

- *Allow owners to delete all messages*: When this option enabled, channel owners can remove all messages in a channel.

- *Allow users to edit their own messages*: When this option is enabled, users can edit their own messages.

- *Allow users to delete their own messages*: When this option is enabled, users can delete their own messages.

- *Allow users to chat privately*: When this option is enabled, users can engage in private chats that are visible only to the people in the chat, instead of everyone on the team.

Creating Teams

IT administrators can control—and decide which users in your organization can create—teams in Teams. Teams creation and control are dependent on Office 365 Group settings. The Teams creation settings that are defined by Office 365 groups will be applied to Teams. Administrators can manage Office 365 groups and can allow/disallow users to create Office 365 groups; those group controls are then applicable to Teams.

Let's discuss how to create a group in Office 365:

1. Open the Office 365 portal by clicking
   https://portal.office.com.

2. Once the portal is open, click Admin to open the Admin Center. Click Groups ➤ Groups in the left navigation pane, and then click Add a Group, as shown in Figure 2-16.

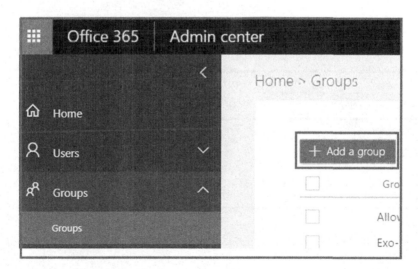

Figure 2-16. *Adding a group*

3. Select the type of group you want to create and then
    type a unique name and Group ID, as shown in
    Figure 2-17.

Figure 2-17. *Creatng a group*

4.   Keep the Send Copies of Group Conversations set to on if you want members to receive messages and calendar items in their own inbox, in addition to the group mailbox. I recommend keep this option on.

Note   You can enable groups to allow external senders after you create the group.

---

5.   Set the Owner. Adding the owner's name is important, because that person can maintain the group.

6.   Click the Add button to create the group.

Controlling the Creation of Teams

If you are looking to create a new group, follow the preceding steps. Controlling the way teams are created is not as straightforward a process, because team creation is dependent on Office 365 groups.

When you disable the ability to create groups in all Office 365 services that will use groups, both administrators and users won't be able to create teams in Microsoft Teams.

There is no native switch that you can turn off to block the creation of teams. You have to use Office 365 groups to block teams creation, because Microsoft Teams uses Office 365 Group settings to create each team. After an user creates a new team, an Office 365 group automatically gets created.

The best way to block group creation in Office 365 is to create a security group. Then, only the people in that security group will be able to create Office 365 groups and Microsoft Teams teams. (Other applications are also dependent on group creation, including Outlook, SharePoint, Yammer, Planner, and StaffHub.) The rest of the people (outside the security group) will be restricted from group creation, and ultimately will be restricted from creating groups in Teams, Outlook, SharePoint, Yammer, Planner, and StaffHub as well.

Caution   Blocking Office 365 group creation will block group creation in Microsoft Teams, Outlook, SharePoint, Yammer, Planner, and StaffHub, so consult with your organization before doing this.

Using a security group to block group creation, as described in the preceding text, is a one-time job. Running similar commands again will result in an error message.

However, note that preventing group creation by using a security group will not block the ability of the following group members to create a group by using the Office 365 Admin Center:

- Global admins

- Mailbox administrator

- Partner, tier 1 support

- Partner, tier2 support

- Directory writers

Let's discuss further how to prevent group creation, which will then block team creation. To control who creates Office 365 groups, you use Windows PowerShell (PowerShell is like the old DOS command interface).

If you have not used PowerShell for Azure Active Directory, you should install the AzureADPreview module for PowerShell (AzureADPreview module, version 2.0.0.137 or later.) Follow these steps:

1. Open Windows PowerShell as an Administrator.

2. Uninstall any previous versions of AzureADPreview, by running the command `Uninstall-Module AzureADPreview`.

3. Install the latest version of AzureADPreview by running the command `Install-Module AzureADPreview`. Type Y to accept the untrusted repository and start installation of AzureADPreview.

Note   Preventing group creation in Office 365, is a group process. You first allow a security group member to create a group, and the rest of the people are prevented from creating a group in Teams or in any other application.

Each organization will have only one security group that can be used to control who can create Office 365 groups. But the Admin user can nest other security groups as members of this group.

For example, the group named Allow Group Creation is the designated security group, and the groups named SharePoint and Exchange Online Users are members of that group.

1. Log in to portal.office.com and choose Select
   Admin ➤ Office 365 Admin Center ➤ Groups. Then
   click Add a Group, as shown in Figure 2-18.

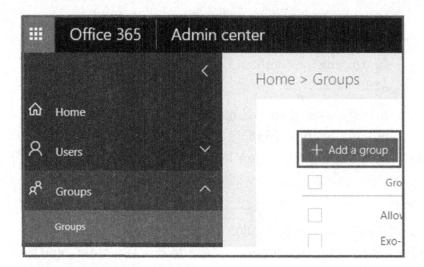

Figure 2-18. *Choosing the Add a Group option*

2. In the Type drop-down list, select Security Group,
   as shown in Figure 2-19. Then give the group a
   meaningful name, such as AllowToCreateGroup.

Figure 2-19. Selecting the type of group

3. Add people or other security groups that you want to be able to create Office 365 groups in your organization.

4. Open PowerShell as Administrator. Type the following commands and then press Enter:

```
Import-Module AzureADPreview
Connect-AzureAD
```

5. In the Sign-in window, enter your Office 365 admin account and password to connect to service, and click Sign In.

    As showed in Figure 2-20, import module for AzureADPreview.

65

```
PS C:\> Import-Module AzureADPreview
PS C:\> Connect-AzureAD

Account                    Environment TenantId                                   TenantDomain    AccountType
-------                    ----------- --------                                   ------------    -----------
bilag@    ware.com AzureCloud  905286fe-0047-422f-8457-93cf5688517e   ware.com User

PS C:\>
```

Figure 2-20. *AzureAD account*

6. Use name of your security group that you created in
    step 2 by using the following syntax:

    ```
    Get-AzureADGroup -SearchString "<Name of your
    security group>"
    ```

    For example, my group name is
    AllowToCreateGroup, so I would run this:

    ```
    Get-AzureADGroup -SearchString "AllowtoCreateGroup
    ```

    This command will display the properties of my
    AllowToCreateGroup security group with an object name.

    As showed in Figure 2-21, verify the Object ID.

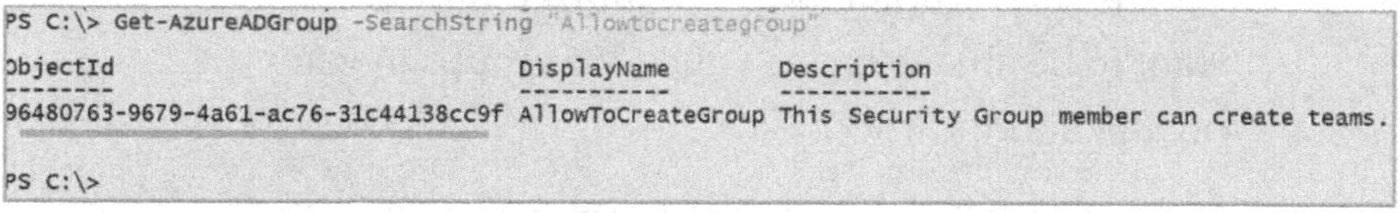

```
PS C:\> Get-AzureADGroup -SearchString "Allowtocreategroup"

ObjectId                               DisplayName       Description
--------                               -----------       -----------
96480763-9679-4a61-ac76-31c44138cc9f AllowToCreateGroup This Security Group member can create teams.

PS C:\>
```

Figure 2-21. *Allowing group creation*

7. Note the ObjectID of your security group in order to
    verify it later.

8. Run this command:

    ```
    $Template = Get-AzureADDirectorySettingTemplate |
    where {$_.DisplayName -eq 'Group.Unified'}
    ```

9. Run this command:

    ```
    $Setting = $Template.CreateDirectorySetting()
    ```

10. Run this command:

    ```
    New-AzureADDirectorySetting -DirectorySetting
    $Setting
    ```

    If you get an error on step 10, skip the rest of the
    steps. The error message means you don't need to
    do step 11.

    Otherwise, upon successful completion, the cmdlet
    returns the ID of the new settings object.

    I did not get an error, so I take the following steps:

11. Run this command:

    ```
    $Setting = Get-AzureADDirectorySetting -Id
    (Get-AzureADDirectorySetting | where -Property
    DisplayName -Value "Group.Unified" -EQ).id
    ```

12. Run this command: `$Setting["EnableGroup`
    `Creation"] = $False`

13. Use this syntax: `$Setting["GroupCreationAllowed`
    `GroupId"] = (Get-AzureADGroup -SearchString`
    `"<Name of your security group>").objectid`

    For example, I named my group
    AllowToCreateGroup, so I would run this command:

    ```
    $Setting["GroupCreationAllowedGroupId"] = (Get-
    AzureADGroup -SearchString "AllowtoCreateGroup").
    objectid
    ```

    As showed in Figure 2-22, allow group creation.

```
PS C:\> $setting = Get-AzureADDirectorySetting -Id (Get-AzureADDirectorySetting | where -Property DisplayName -Value "Group.Unified" -EQ).id
PS C:\> $setting["EnableGroupCreation"] = $false
PS C:\> $setting["GroupCreationAllowedGroupId"] = (Get-AzureADGroup -SearchString "AllowToCreateGroup").objectid
PS C:\>
```

Figure 2-22. *Allowing one group and blocking the rest*

14. Run this command:

    Set-AzureADDirectorySetting -Id (Get-
    AzureADDirectorySetting | where -Property DisplayName
    -Value "Group.Unified" -EQ).id -DirectorySetting $Setting

15. To verify that your security group *can* create groups,
    and everyone else in your organization *can't*, run
    this command:

    (Get-AzureADDirectorySetting).Values

    The result should look like this (but with the ID
    value for your security group—this is where you
    need to be able to recognize it).

    As showed in Figure 2-23, Verify Group Creation
    allowed group.

```
PS C:\> (Get-AzureADDirectorySetting).values

Name                             Value
----                             -----
CustomBlockedWordsList
EnableMSStandardBlockedWords     False
ClassificationDescriptions
DefaultClassification
PrefixSuffixNamingRequirement
AllowGuestsToBeGroupOwner        False
AllowGuestsToAccessGroups        True
GuestUsageGuidelinesUrl
GroupCreationAllowedGroupId      96480763-9679-4a61-ac76-31c44138cc9f
AllowToAddGuests                 True
UsageGuidelinesUrl
ClassificationList
EnableGroupCreation              False

PS C:\>
```

Figure 2-23. *Verify Group Creation allowed group*

The group ID is the ID of the group that can create teams.

Preparing Your Organization for Teams

Planning and Preparation organization for Microsoft Teams is highly essential phase, planning include network planning is important for Microsoft Teams because if a network is not planned correctly, the users' Teams experience will be degraded. Teams is heavily dependent on the network, especially when it comes to real-time communication traffic. Real-time traffic occurs when one-to-one audio/video calls, conference calls, and desktop sharing happen. Teams also has non-real-time traffic such as Presence, Chat, and file sharing.

Office 365 applications usually communicate only to the cloud services in which the backed infrastructure is. Everything goes in one direction. For example, when e-mail is sent, it goes to an Exchange Online server in the cloud, and the uploaded file goes to the SharePoint Online cloud.

However, Microsoft Teams uses real-time communication. For instance, when User A calls User B (and these users are sitting in different offices or locations), the Teams client doesn't want to send traffic to Teams (remote cloud) services. Instead, Teams prefers to send traffic directly, from peer to peer—from User A's computer to User B's computer (and vice versa). One to one audio calls, video calls, and desktop-sharing traffic travels directly whenever possible in order to have better quality.

The following are the traffic forms generated by Teams:

- Data traffic between the Office 365 online environment and the Microsoft Teams client (signaling, presence, chat, file upload and download, OneNote synchronization)

- Peer-to-peer real-time communications traffic (audio, video, desktop sharing)

- Conferencing real-time communications traffic (audio, video, desktop sharing)

So, when network planning happens, the IT administrator has to try to keep direct traffic within the corporate network whenever possible, in order to have better quality. If a firewall/ proxy is deployed on the corporate network (for example, between building A and B, or between office A and B), Teams traffic will not travel directly because of the firewall interference. Then the Teams client will send traffic to cloud services for relay, by using a cloud relay service. However, the network path will be longer, with an extra hop, because it has to go first to Office 365 cloud services, via the public Internet. As a result, quality will suffer, so Teams prefers to send one-to-one call traffic directly instead of using a relay.

If a conference call or meeting involves more than two users, Teams always sends traffic to cloud services that have conferencing services; these mix the audio and then send it to the participant. So direct media is applied to one-to-one calls but not meetings.

For real-time communication, Teams prefers User Datagram Protocol (UDP) over Transmission Control Protocol (TCP). TCP is great, because if any packet gets lost, TCP will retransmit the lost packet. However, this is not good for real-time traffic such as audio; if any audio packets get lost, we are not really interested in waiting to resend the lost packet, because in real-time communication, the packet has to reach its destination as soon as possible. If a packet is lost, then it doesn't matter for 20 ml audio Teams can recovers from Teams intelligence media stack. UDP is always better for quality. If UDP is not allowed, Teams uses TCP and UDP protocols for media traffic.

Microsoft has list of IP addresses, fully qualified domain names (FQDNs), and ports that need to be open as part of network requirements for Teams. It is important to visit `https://docs.microsoft.com/en-us/MicrosoftTeams/office-365-urls-ip-address-ranges` and go through this list. Work with your network and InfoSec team to allow the listed IPs, FQDNs, and ports.

Microsoft recommends subscribing via RSS feeds (`https://go.microsoft.com/fwlink/p/?linkid=236301`) to receive notifications when endpoints are updated or changed.

Once you allow the required IPs, FQDNs, and ports, it is very important to monitor and validate that the Teams features are working the way they should be. Microsoft updates these lists from time to time, so it is important to subscribe the RSS feeds and allow new listed IPs, FQDNs, and ports. Otherwise, all the Microsoft Teams features will not work as expected.

Microsoft Teams traffic will flow between the Microsoft Teams clients directly for one-to-one contacts, and traffic will flow between the Office 365 environment for meeting scenarios. To ensure optimal traffic flow, traffic must be allowed to flow between the corporate network segments in local area networks and wide area networks, as well as between the network sites and Office 365. Not opening the correct ports or actively blocking specific ports will lead to a degraded experience.

Note   Currently, meetings are supported on iOS and Android mobile devices, but not on Windows Phone (support for Windows Phone is coming in late 2018).

Network Requirements

For an optimal experience with real-time media within Microsoft Teams, you must meet the networking requirements for Office 365.

The two defining network segments (Client to Microsoft Edge, and Customer Edge to Microsoft Edge) must meet the requirements listed in Table 2-1.

Table 2-1. Latency information

Value	Client to Microsoft Edge	Customer Edge to Microsoft Edge
Latency (one way)	< 50 ms	< 30 ms
Latency (RTT, or round-trip time)	< 100 ms	< 60 ms
Burst packet loss	< 10% during any 200 ms interval	< 1% during any 200 ms interval
Packet loss	< 1% during any 15 s interval	< 0.1% during any 15 s interval
Packet inter-arrival jitter	< 30 ms during any 15 s interval	< 15ms during any 15 s interval
Packet reorder	< 0.05% out-of-order packets	< 0.01% out-of-order packets

Bandwidth Requirements

Network Planner is an online tool that allows you to configure your network. You can indicate the number of sites and the users, and the tool will tell you the amount of bandwidth you should plan for.

If the required bandwidth is not available, the media stack inside Microsoft Teams will degrade the quality of the audio/video session to accommodate for that lower amount of available bandwidth, impacting the quality of the call/meeting. The Microsoft Teams client will attempt to prioritize the quality of audio over the quality of video. It is therefore extremely important to have the expected bandwidth available.

Table 2-2 shows required bandwidth for Teams modality.

Table 2-2. *Required bandwidth for Teams modality*

Activity	Download Bandwidth	Upload Bandwidth	Traffic Flow
Peer-to-peer audio call	0.1 Mb	0.1 Mb	Client <> Client
Peer-to-peer video call (full screen)	4 Mb	4 Mb	Client <> Client
Peer-to-peer desktop sharing (1920 * 1080 resolution)	4 Mb	4 Mb	Client <> Client
Two-participant meeting	4 Mb	4 Mb	Client <> Office 365
Three-participant meeting	8 Mb	6.5 Mb	Client <> Office 365
Four-participant meeting	5.5 Mb	4 Mb	Client <> Office 365
Five-participant meeting or more	6 Mb	1.5 Mb	Client <> Office 365

Bandwidth calculations for Microsoft Teams are complex. To help with this, a calculator has been created. To access the calculator, go to http://aka.ms/bwcalc/. Above table shows required network bandwidth for each modality including one-to-one call, meeting etc.

Additional Network Considerations

The network is the backbone of any real-time communication product. Therefore, in addition to bandwidth considerations and network improvements, there are other considerations. These factors are described in this section.

External Name Resolution

Make sure that all the client computers running Microsoft Teams can resolve external Domain Name System (DNS) queries to discover the services provided by Office 365.

NAT Pool Size

When multiple users or devices access Office 365 by using network address translation (NAT) or port address translation (PAT), you need to ensure that the devices hidden behind each publicly routable IP address do not exceed the supported number.

To mitigate this risk, ensure that adequate public IP addresses are assigned to the NAT pools to prevent port exhaustion. Port exhaustion will cause internal end users and devices to face issues when connecting to Office 365 services.

Intrusion Detection and Prevention

If the environment has an intrusion detection system (IDS) or intrusion prevention system (IPS) deployed for an extra layer of security for outbound connections, ensure that any traffic with a destination to Office 365 URLs is whitelisted.

Best Practices

The following are network best practices:

- *Allow required connections* for IPs, FQDNs, and ports.

- *Allow local Internet breakouts*: Whenever possible, use Internet breakouts. This is difficult for organizations because they use MPLS networks to connect branch offices and use Internet breakouts from central offices. However, Teams wants to send traffic as quickly as possible to Office 365 services, so local Internet breakouts work better for Teams. Teams traffic routed internally will add delays and latency.

- *Avoid proxy servers*: Most companies use proxy servers, which must be bypassed, as proxy servers will add delays and to some extent drop UDP packets. When a proxy server sits between a client and the Office 365 data centers, media might be forced over TCP instead of UDP, which would degrade media quality.

If your networking and security policies require Office 365 traffic to flow through a proxy server, make sure that the preceding requirements are already met before deploying Microsoft Teams into production. (Review "Proxy Servers for Skype for Business Online" for more details, at `https://support.office.com/en-us/article/Proxy-Servers-for-Skype-for-Business-Online-7acaf2c2-35fa-490f-84cd-822e446e0fc7?ui=en-US&rs=en-US&ad=US`.)

- *Plan network connectivity for bandwidth and quality*: Bandwidth planning is another important step in preparing for Teams. If the required bandwidth is not available, the media stack inside Microsoft Teams will degrade the quality of the audio/video session to accommodate for that lower amount of available bandwidth, impacting the quality of the call/meeting. The Microsoft Teams client will attempt to prioritize the quality of audio over the quality of video. It is therefore extremely important to have the expected bandwidth available.

- *Perform testing and validation after implementation*: After meeting the preceding requirements, it is important to validate those requirements. Make sure you have the required bandwidth, access to all required IP addresses, and the correct ports opened, and are meeting the performance requirements for real-time media.

If network requirements are not met, end users will not have an optimal experience with Microsoft Teams because of bad quality connections during calls and meetings.

Enhancing Productivity with Bots

Microsoft Teams is a chat-based workspace with persistent chat, conversations, one-to-one calls, meetings, file storage, and more. Teams has many more capabilities. To use Teams effectively with all those capabilities, using a bot is good option. What is a bot?

Bots are preconfigured and automated programs that are set up to respond to queries or give updates and notifications about things you find interesting or want to stay informed about. Bots don't have moods like humans, and they are always available, which is beneficial.

In Microsoft Teams, you can chat with a bot just as if it were a person. In Teams, a built-in bot called T-Bot is designed to chat one-on-one. Bots are ready whenever you have questions about Microsoft Teams, or if you need help with channels, calls, meetings, task management, scheduling, or polling. Other bots can be added to your teams in Microsoft Teams, so they'll be able to post messages in channels. That way, bots can keep your entire team up-to-date without your manual involvement. A bot is always online and does not have a mood message.

T-Bot is a useful bot that's available in Teams to help users learn how to use Microsoft Teams! Ask a question or type a keyword or phrase into a chat with T-Bot, as shown in Figure 2-24, and it will find the answer.

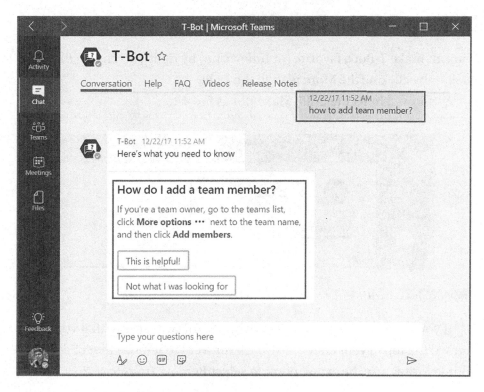

Figure 2-24. *T-Bot answers questions*

T-Bot is mainly used to answer questions about Microsoft Teams. There is no command list that you can call up to see what T-Bot can do. There is also no way to write new commands for T-Bot.

Making T-Bot a Favorite?

You can make T-Bot a favorite (or unfavorite) by right-clicking on the chat itself or by clicking the More icon to the right.

As showed in Figure 2-25, Make Bot as favorite.

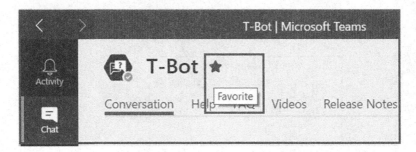

Figure 2-25. *Making T-Bot a favorite*

If you are adding T-Bot to your favorites, this will ensure that your chat stays at the top of your chat list. If you ever want to remove that chat from your favorites, use the same menu to select Remove from Favorites.

Disabling T-Bot

T-Bot is designed to help you to become comfortable using Microsoft Teams, and there is no way to disable T-Bot entirely. However, you can disable tips and tricks sent by T-Bot, if you decide you no longer want to receive them.

Search T-Bot chat and then click the More icon next to the T-Bot chat. That opens a menu with the option to Disable Tips and Tricks, as shown in Figure 2-26.

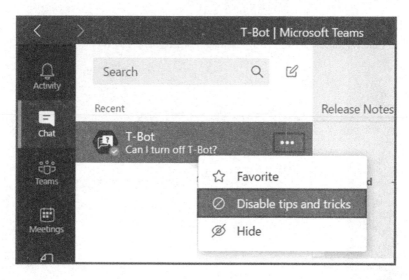

Figure 2-26. *Disabling T-Bot tips and tricks*

After you select that option, T-Bot will talk to you only if you send it a question or comment. If you ever want to turn tips and tricks back on, go to the same menu and select Enable Tips and Tricks.

Discovering Bots That Have Been Added

Now, you might ask, how do you check which bots have been added to a team? That's simple; here are the steps:

1. Click the More icon next to the team name. Then select View Team or Manage Team, as shown in Figure 2-27.

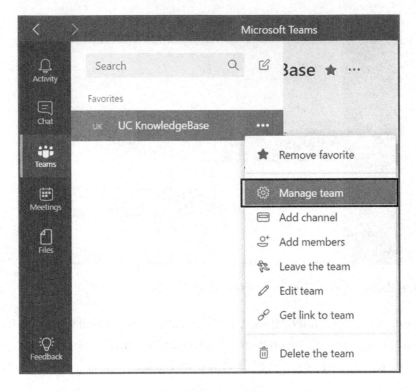

Figure 2-27. *Choosing the bot Manage Team option*

2. Click the Bots tab. You'll see a list of bots that have been added to that team, as shown in Figure 2-28.

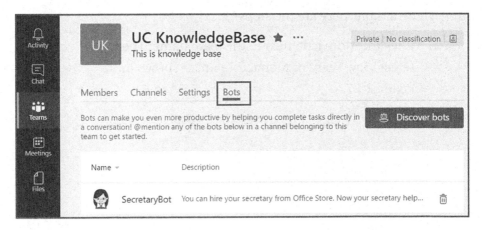

Figure 2-28. *Discovering bots that have been added to the team*

You can also click Discover Bots at the top-right corner of your team view to see the bots that are available in Microsoft Teams.

To the right of the bot name, you will see *Added* if the bot has already been added to your team. A plus sign (+) indicates that you can add that bot to your team.

For example, Figure 2-29 shows that SecretaryBot has been added to my teams.

Figure 2-29. *SecretaryBot has been added to Teams*

So far, 30 built-in bots are available to add to any teams and to avail you of their help.

Currently T-Bot chat queries and responses are supported in the following four languages:

- English (US)

- French

- German

- Spanish

Adding a Bot to Your Team

As you've seen, discovering a bot is easy. To add a bot, you click in the search bar and choose the Discover Bots option at the bottom of the list. From here, you can add bots to your one-to-one conversations and teams. Another way to add bots to a team is to click the More icon next to your team name, select View Team, and then click the Bots tab. From here, click Discover Bots to find bots and add them to your team.

Remember, though, you can add bots to teams only if your team owner has enabled team members to add bots to Teams.

Select the desired bot and click the plus sign (+). A new page opens, and then click Add. For example, in Figure 2-30, SurveyMonkey has been selected and added.

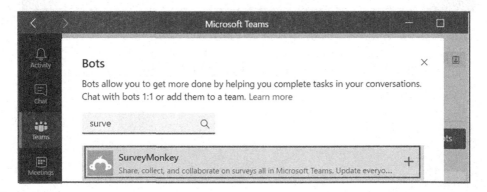

Figure 2-30. *Adding a selected bot*

Now you can see that the SurveyMonkey bot has been added to my team, as shown in Figure 2-31.

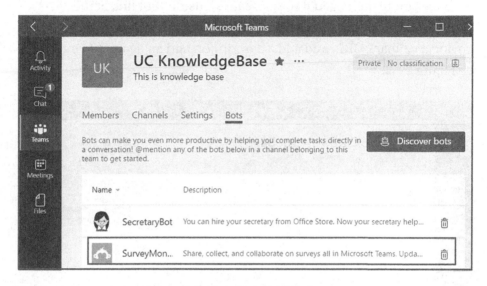

Figure 2-31. *SurveyMonkey has been added*

Using Custom Bots

Custom bots are great way to increase productivity. Teams has many built-in bots available. However, if your requirements are not fulfilled with existing bots, you can create custom bots to integrate the service you want into Microsoft Teams so it's usable in any of your channels.

For example, you can create a custom bot to send a daily Teams activity or weather report, or to remind you to break for lunch. To get a better idea of how to use our framework to create your own bots, go to https://aka.ms/microsoftteamscustombots.

Creating your own personalized bots and adding them to a team is quick and easy. And if you're handy with code, you can create your own custom bot! For more information about how to do that, go to https://msdn.microsoft.com/en-us/microsoft-teams/botscreate.

Open Teams and click the teams list. Then click the More icon next to a team. Select the View Team option and navigate to the Bots tab.

Once you're there, you'll see a Create a Custom Bot link at the bottom-right corner of the screen. Click through, and then name your bot, provide a callback URL, and add a description and an avatar (if you like); see Figure 2-32.

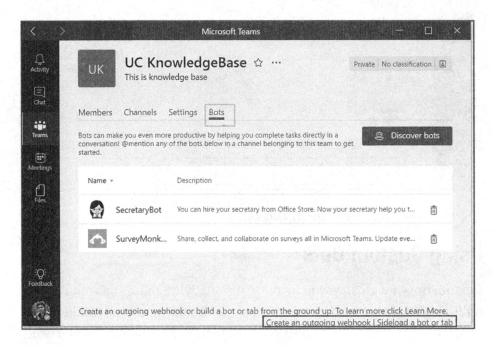

Figure 2-32. *Custom bot*

Click the "Create an outgoing webhook | Sideload a bot or tab" option at the bottom of the page.

The next page allows you to configure the way your bot appears in channels:

- *Name*: This will show up as the bot's title and is what users will use to @mention the bot.

- *Callback URL*: The endpoint that will receive messages from Teams.

- *Description*: A detailed string that will show up in the profile card and in the team-level App dashboard.

- *Avatar*: The optional display picture of the custom bot.

Figure 2-33 shows these options.

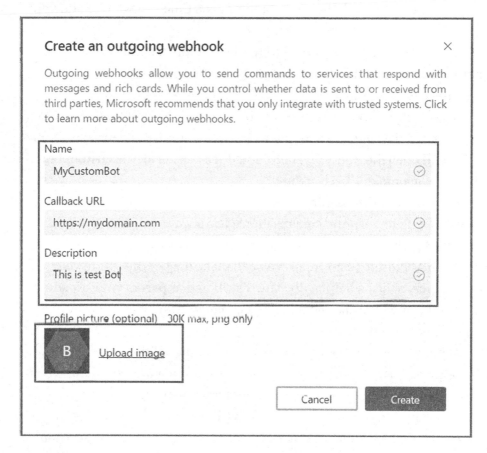

Figure 2-33. *Setting custom bot details*

Adding a Custom Bot

Once you add a custom bot to a specific team, you won't be able to chat with it automatically from other teams. What you can do is set up a custom bot in another team that integrates with the same service. However, you will need to go through the setup process each time you want to add your custom bot to a new team.

To chat with a custom bot in a channel, simply @mention the bot by name in a message. For now, you can @mention and chat only with bots in channels, not one-on-one.

To see the custom bots that have been added to a certain team, click the More icon next to the team name in your teams list. Then, select View team and open the Bots tab. There, you'll see a list of all the custom bots that your teammates have created!

Bot appears just like any other team member you interact with, in a channel or in one-to-one conversations. It is always online and doesn't have bad moods.

With Microsoft Teams apps, you can make the bot the star of your experience, or just a helper. Bots are distributed as part of your broader app package, which can include other capabilities such as tabs or messaging extensions.

If your bot is the star, be sure to take advantage of the tabs capability as well. Use this rich web view to present accompanying experiences and information that helps your users best interact with your service.

You can easily see all custom bots available in Teams. Open Teams and then click the More icon next to the team name in your teams list. Then, select View Team and open the Bots tab within that view. There, you'll see a list of all the custom bots that you or your teammates have created.

Deploying and Updating Clients

Microsoft Teams clients are available for all platforms, including web clients that don't have a thick client installed, desktop clients for the Windows platform, Mac clients for macOS, and mobility clients for iOS, Android, and Windows Phone; see Figure 2-34.

Figure 2-34. *Teams clients available*

- You can download the Teams application installer (.exe) from `https://teams.microsoft.com/downloads` and then click on install option.

- For the web client, users can browse to `https://teams.microsoft.com` to access Teams without installing it on their computer.

Performing Bulk Deployment

There are few options for bulk deployment of Teams:

- Share the download URL over e-mail communication. You can share the Teams desktop or Mac download URL and let users complete the installation. Installing a Teams client does not require Admin permission.

- Share the location and batch file.

    - Using share location option, administrator can download teams.exe file and installer.bat file to share location and allow end-users to download and install themself.

    - Create a batch file using the details that follow in the next subsection and save file with the installer.bat name.

- Use SCCM and Group Policy to deploy the Teams client.

Microsoft Teams Client Rollout Using MSI

Microsoft has provided an MSI package for Teams clients. This MSI package is available in both 32-bit and 64-bit format. For a Teams client rollout, the IT administrator can leverage SCCM, or Group Policy, or any third-party distribution mechanisms, as in any other application deployment. IT admins can use Teams files to remotely deploy Teams so that users do not have to manually download the Teams app on their machine. When the client is deployed, Teams will auto launch for all users who sign in on that machine.

The following are prerequisites for Teams client deployment:

- .NET framework 4.5 or later

- Windows 7 operating system or later

- 32 GB of disk space for each user profile (recommended)

The following are steps to complete Teams client deployment:

1. Complete the Teams client prerequisites, including installing the Windows 7 operating system as a minimum, .the NET Framework 4.5 as a minimum, and 32 GB of free space.

2. Download the MSI package by using the following URLs:

   - 32-bit: `http://aka.ms/teams32bitmsi`

   - 64-bit: `http://aka.ms/teams64bitmsi`

3. Copy the Teams client MSI package to the end user's program files, so whenever a user logs in to the machine, the installer will be launched and the Teams client will be installed.

If a machine already has a Teams client installed, the MSI installer process will skip for that user.

How do you uninstall and reinstall a Teams client?

When you deploy Teams through the MSI installer, it will track the installation status in case the user uninstalls Teams. Then you can redeploy the Teams client on a specific machine by following these steps:

1. Uninstall the Teams app installed for every user profile on a particular machine.

2. After uninstalling, delete the directory recursively under `%localappdata%\Microsoft\Teams\`.

3. Redeploy the MSI package to that particular machine.

Note   Microsoft Teams installation does not require Admin permission, so end users can install a Teams client without Admin permission.

Summary

This chapter will help you enable and configure Microsoft Teams appropriately. Teams has many tenant-wide settings, and each setting has a different usage. After setting up the tenant, you must control the creation of teams by using Office 365 groups, because by default everyone can create a Team, but you can control this behavior. Finally, deploy a Teams client on each computer to use Teams efficiently.

CHAPTER 3

Managing and Controlling the Teams Experience

In this chapter, you'll learn about provisioning and administrating teams with guest access. This chapter covers the following topics:

1. Provisioning and managing users

2. Administration of teams and channels

3. Managing and controlling teams via custom policies

4. Managing guest access to teams

5. Using PowerShell to manage the Teams experience

Provisioning and Managing Users

Provisioning users for teams is dependent on the tenant level switch for Teams. When this switch turns on, Teams is enabled for all users; and when the switch is off, Teams is disabled for all users and types.

Microsoft may remove this switch in the future because it is not a preferred way to provide user-level control. As soon as the IT administrator sets up the Office 365 tenant, Microsoft Teams is enabled by default for all users.

© Balu N Ilag 2018
B.N. Ilag, *Introducing Microsoft Teams*, https://doi.org/10.1007/978-1-4842-3567-6_3

The Teams license is assigned by default with all Office 365 license plans (which has Teams) to users when Office 365 license assigned However, the administrator can manually turn off a Teams license in order to turn off user access for Teams. (For more details on which plans include a Teams license, refer to "License Requirements" in Chapter 1.)

Enabling User Access

As an IT administrator, you can control user-level access to Microsoft Teams by using licenses. However, there is no switch that you can turn on or off for a Teams user. As I mentioned earlier, you can enable or disable Teams on a per user basis by assigning or removing the Microsoft Teams product license. Microsoft Teams user-level licenses are managed directly through the Office 365 Admin Center user management interfaces. As an IT administrator, you can assign licenses to new users when new user accounts are created, or to users with existing accounts.

Note   To control user licenses by using the Office 365 Admin Center, you must have Global Admin or User Management Admin group permission.

To assign and enable licenses, follow these steps:

1. Log in to Office 365 portal (`https://portal.office.com/adminportal/home#/homepage`).

2. Choose Users ➤ Active Users.

3. Find a specific user, and then select that user to see the properties.

4. Select Product Licenses and then click Edit.

For example, for the user Balu Ilag, edit the Product License and enable/disable Teams (see Figure 3-1).

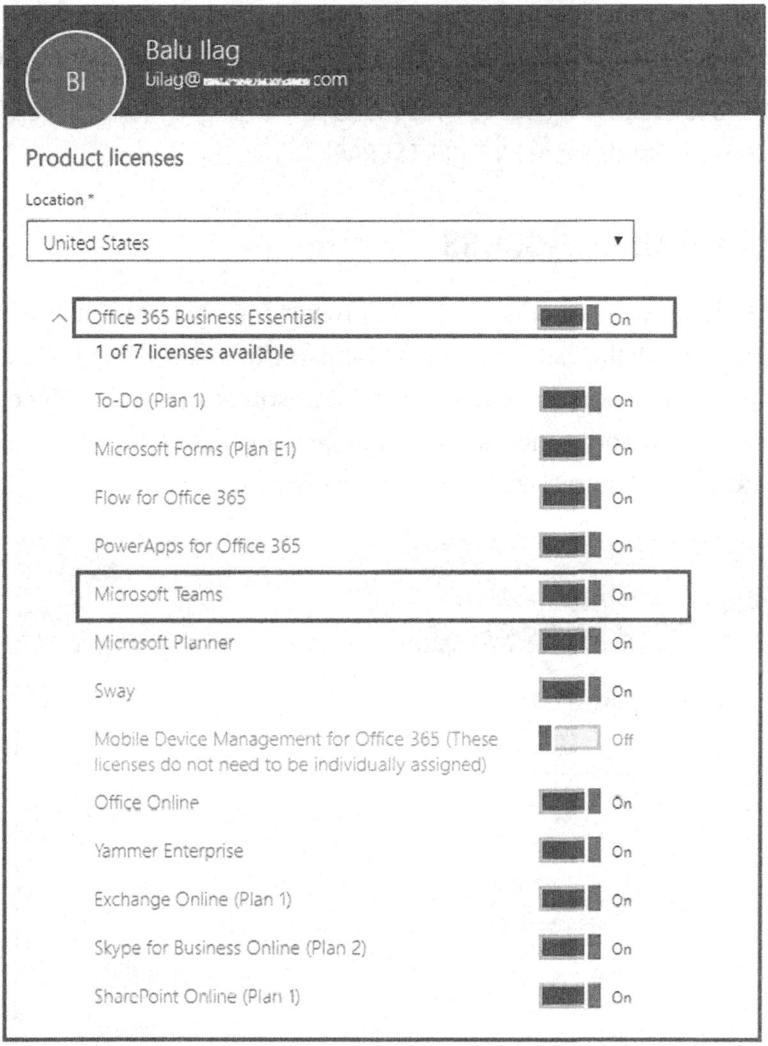

Figure 3-1. *Assigning a license to a user*

You can also use PowerShell commands to assign or revoke a license to an individual user. The following command assigns a license:

```
Cmdlet: Set-MsolUserLicense -UserPrincipalName "<Account>"
-AddLicenses "<AccountSkuId>"
```

In the following example, I'm assigning the mydomain:ENTERPRISEPACK (Office 365 Enterprise E3) license to the user account bilag@mydomain.com:

```
Set-MsolUserLicense -UserPrincipalName "bilag@mydomain.com"
-AddLicenses "mydomain:ENTERPRISEPACK"
```

Disabling User Access

To disable Teams, you can disable the Microsoft Teams user license. After the license is disabled, the user's access to Microsoft Teams will be prevented, and the user will no longer be able to see Microsoft Teams in the Office 365 app launcher and home page and will unable to log in to Microsoft Teams.

As showed in Figure 3-2, Disable Teams license.

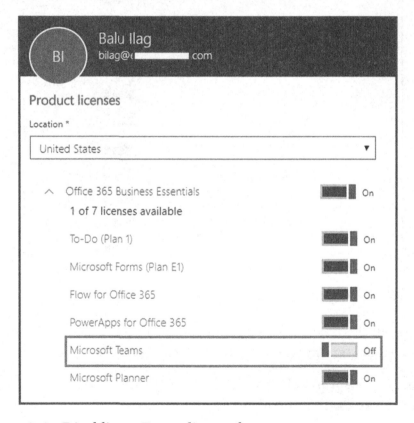

Figure 3-2. *Disabling a Teams license for a user*

94

To remove licenses from an existing user account, you use this command:

```
Set-MsolUserLicense -UserPrincipalName <Account>
-RemoveLicenses "<AccountSkuId1>", "<AccountSkuId2>"
```

The following, for example, removes the mydomain:ENTERPRISEPACK (Office 365 Enterprise E3) license from the user account bilag@mydomain.com:

```
Set-MsolUserLicense -UserPrincipalName bilag@mydomain.com
-RemoveLicenses "mydomain:ENTERPRISEPACK"
```

Administration of Teams and Channels

Microsoft *teams* are a collection of people, content, and tools surrounding different projects and jobs within an organization.

Channels are dedicated sections within a team that keep conversations organized by specific topics, projects, and disciplines that work for your team. Channels organize a team's conversations, content, and tools around specific topics. You can think of a team as a project and a channel as a single task under that project. Figure 3-3 illustrates this concept.

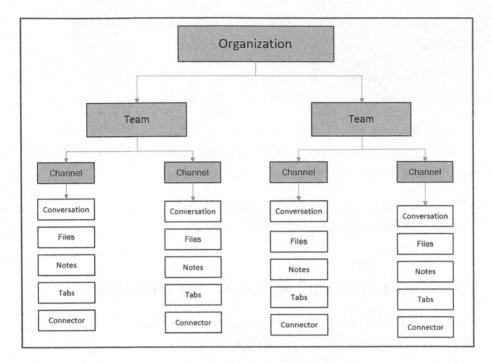

Figure 3-3. *The flow between teams and channels*

If you look at this flow chart, you'll see that the organization at the top has various teams. Each team has multiple channels. Each channel has separate conversations, files, notes, tabs, and connectors. So you can treat each team as a separate project, and each channel under a team can be considered a single task with conversations, files, notes, tabs, and connectors.

Creating a Team

Let's discuss teams in more detail. While creating a team, you must add team members (team members can be added later also). Each team can have up to 2,500 members and 100 owners.

What is the difference between a team owner and member? The distinction between owner and team member is required, because the owner will have complete control over teams, whereas a member can do only certain things.

Team owners can do things like add new members and add other owners, rename the team, delete the team, or edit the settings for the team. You have to be careful when promoting a member/user to a team owner, because an owner can even delete teams.

When a team is created, an Office 365 group will be created in Office 365, which includes a shared Outlook inbox and calendar, a SharePoint site and document library, a OneNote notebook, and Planner.

Note   If you already have an established Office 365 group, it's best to activate Microsoft Teams on your existing group instead of creating one from scratch.

Here are the steps to create a new team:

1. Log in to Microsoft Teams. In the left navigation pane, select Teams.

2. In the middle pane, select Add Team, and then click Create Team, as shown in Figure 3-4.

Figure 3-4. *Creating a team*

3. After you click Create Team, enter a name and a description for your team, as shown in Figure 3-5. Then select Public or Private, edit the default security setting if needed, and click Next.

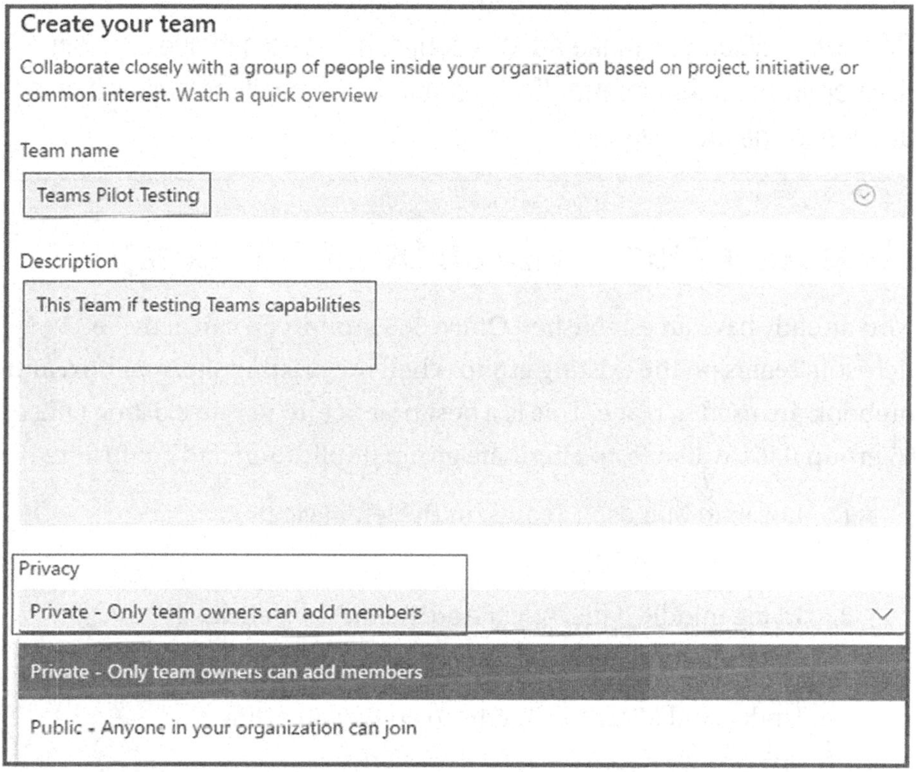

Create your team

Collaborate closely with a group of people inside your organization based on project, initiative, or common interest. Watch a quick overview

Team name

Teams Pilot Testing

Description

This Team if testing Teams capabilities

Privacy

Private - Only team owners can add members

Private - Only team owners can add members

Public - Anyone in your organization can join

Figure 3-5. *Selling options for your team*

Note   A private team is invitation-only. In contrast, people can see a public team and can join it without an invitation.

---

4. In the Member box, enter the name or e-mail of a person you would like to add, select the person's name, and then select Add. Repeat this step until you have added everyone you would like to add as team member.

Caution   When you make a team public, all users can see and join it. Keep in mind that information in a public team will be accessible to anyone in the organization.

Integrating Teams with an Office 365 Group

If you already have an established Office 365 group, you can activate Microsoft Teams on the existing group. Then the existing site, mailbox, and notebook are used in place. This is a best practice, to use an existing Office 365 group if it's available, to eliminate group duplication and confusion:

1. Log in to Microsoft Teams. In the left navigation pane, select Teams.

2. In the middle pane, select Add Team. Then click Create Team.

3. Under Add Microsoft Teams to an Existing Office 365 Group, select Yes. Add the Microsoft Teams functionality, and then click Next.

4. Select your team, and then click Choose Team. You will be directed to your new workspace in Microsoft Teams.

Understanding Channels

As you've learned, channels are dedicated sections within a team to keep conversations organized by specific topics, projects, and disciplines. Channels organize a team's conversations, content, and tools around specific topics. As stated earlier, you can think of a team as a project and a channel as asingle task under that project.

Each team begins with a General channel, which is default. You, as the owner of the team, cannot delete the General channel. You can create other channels for whatever topics you want. You can modify or delete newly added channels in the team or keep channels safe in an archive. When you delete a channel, you lose all the conversation data in that channel. If a topic will be around for a while, you can create channel for it and add conversations on that topic; when you're finished, you can keep the channel archived.

Conversations shared in channels are visible to all of the members of your team. Anyone who is a member of the team can create channels under the same team. Remember, all teams have the default General channel, which cannot be deleted (see Figure 3-6).

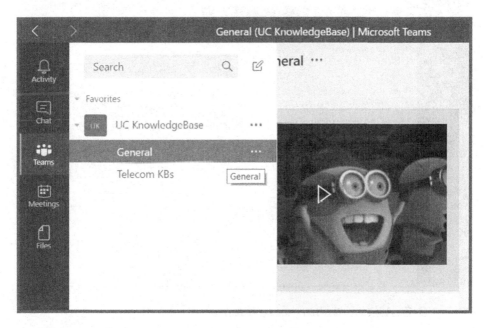

Figure 3-6. *The General channel for a team*

Using a Channel Effectively

In this section, you'll first learn how to create a channel. The process is easy: select Teams in the left navigation pane, select the More icon, which looks like an ellipsis (...), to the right of the team name, and then click Add Channel. Figure 3-7 illlustrates the process.

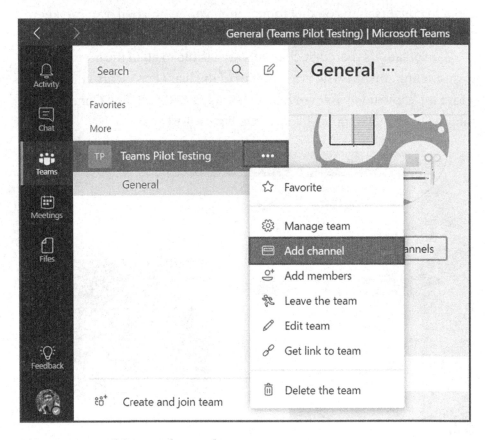

Figure 3-7. *Adding a channel to a team*

Then you provide the channel name and use for selected topic.

You can make your channel a favorite. To do so, click the star to the right of the channel name. When you make a channel a favorite, it will remain visible.

If the topic (channel) is important to you, you might want it to be at the top of the list of channels. In this case, you should follow the channel: select the ellipsis (...) to the right of the team name, and then click Follow This Channel. You will receive alerts for all activity on all channels you follow.

Tip   Following a busy channel is not a good idea, because you will receive a notification every time someone updates any note or comment related to that channel.

To e-mail a channel, select the ellipsis (...) to the right of the team name, and then select Get Email Address, as shown in Figure 3-8. Use the channel e-mail address to send e-mail to the channel you're your outlook.

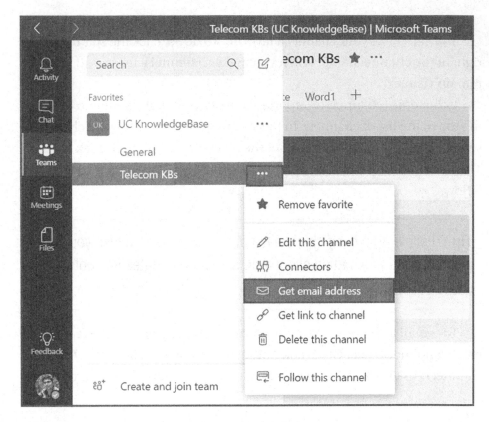

Figure 3-8. *Getting e-mail for a channel*

The e-mail address will look like Telecom KBs - UC KnowledgeBase, `075f1b3e.mydomain.com@amer.teams.ms`.

Having a Video Meeting

Participating in a video meeting is another good way to interact with coworkers or team members. You can directly start a video meeting from a group conversation.

From a conversation, click the Meet Now icon. This meeting will then happen on the channel, and any member can see this meeting and participate in it.

Meet Now, shown in Figure 3-9, is useful when you want to have an immediate call with anyone on the team who wants to join. Alternatively, you can select Schedule a Meeting to meet at a later time.

If you have more than five participants in a video call, you will see the four most recent speakers in the video, which will be small and in the right-hand corner.

Figure 3-9. *Video call option*

Scheduling a Meeting

You can also schedule a meeting by selecting Meetings ➤ Schedule a Meeting. Scheduling a meeting is the best option for meeting with participants who are not all members of the same team.

The Teams meeting calendar is integrated with the Outlook calendar, so you will see all your Outlook or Skype meetings in your Teams calendar. You can schedule a meeting in Teams just as you would schedule a meeting in Outlook—for example, like adding a conference room or making a call if you want to.

You can also add a channel to the meeting. If it is a private meeting, don't add a channel to the meeting; otherwise, all members of that channel will be added to meeting. If a meeting conversation is added to a channel, you can find the meeting and read its details in the channel.

Scheduling a meeting and invite people for meeting, as shown in Figure 3-10.

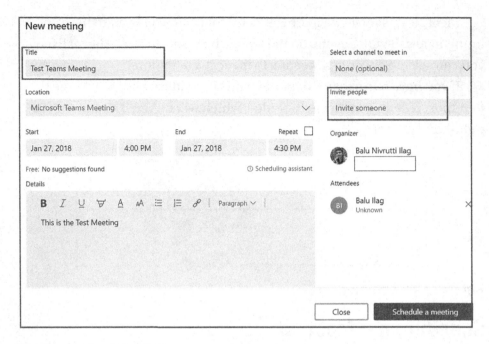

Figure 3-10. Scheduling a meeting

Working with Tabs in a Channel

Every channel has three default tabs: Conversations, Files, and Wiki, as shown in Figure 3-11:

- *Conversations*: You can use this tab to have interactive conversations with your team. You will be able to use all chat features in a conversation.

- *Files*: This tab is useful when you want to share documents or files within a channel. You can upload, view, and share documents through this tab. These documents and files are stored in your team's SharePoint document library. This integration with SharePoint Online is seamless; you will be able to view, upload, and share these documents.

- *Wiki*: This tab is useful for taking notes, @mentioning your team members, or drafting and editing content in real time. The Wiki tab enables you to have an interactive note-taking experience. You can type a note in Wiki, create new sections, and @mention people; everyone can edit content in the Wiki tab in real time.

Figure 3-11. *Accessing tabs in a channel*

In addition to these default tabs, you can create custom tabs as needed. You'll explore both the default tabs and custom tabs in this section.

Conversations tTab

To start a conversation, you have to enter a message in the Start a Conversation box and then press Enter (or click the Send icon). Your message will then be posted in the channel, and all team members will be able to see the message. You can start a private conversation as well with any member, as a one-on-one conversation.

To respond to an existing message, use the Reply option. Justclick Reply below the message and then enter a reply to create a threaded message.

You can @mention a specific member. Simply type @MemberName with your message, and that team member will receive an alert.

Using message options, you can save, delete, like, and add some flair to your messages with an emoji, Giphy file, or sticker.

To find a message, enter a keyword in the Search box and then select the Conversations tab.

Files Tab

All files shared in a team channel conversation can be found in the channel's Files tab, shown in Figure 3-12.

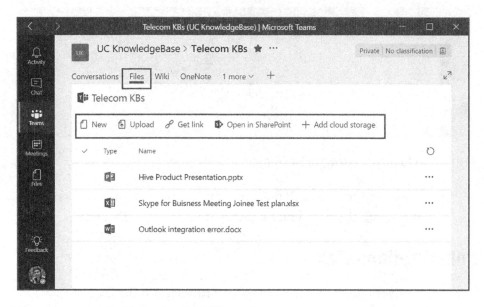

Figure 3-12. *Options in the Files tab*

You can also upload files directly to the Files tab. In addition, you can start a conversation about a file by opening the file in Teams and selecting Start Conversation in the upper right.

To view your Microsoft Team files in SharePoint where they are stored, select Open in SharePoint.

Wiki Tab

As I mentioned earlier, each team channel has a Wiki tab to use for taking notes or drafting and editing content in real time. It's a text editor that lets you @mention team members and leave or reply to comments. The Wiki tab, shown in Figure 3-13, is great for informal notes.

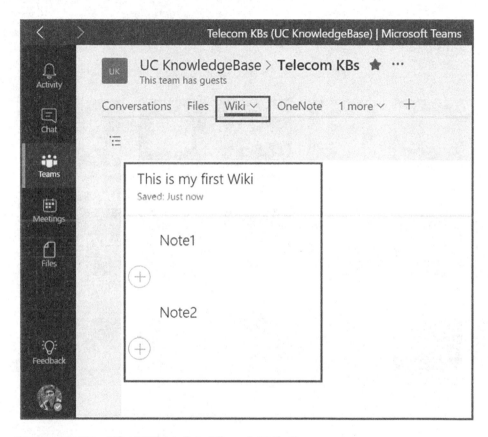

Figure 3-13. *The Wiki tab with a detailed message*

Every Wiki topic contains sections, and each section supports its own conversation.

Wiki content is stored and governed in SharePoint Online.

Custom Tabs

Apart from the Conversations, Files, and Wiki tabs, you can add custom tabs that will allow you to integrate tools and services. You or your team can use custom tabs right in a channel. A few popular examples of custom tabs are shown in Figure 3-14.

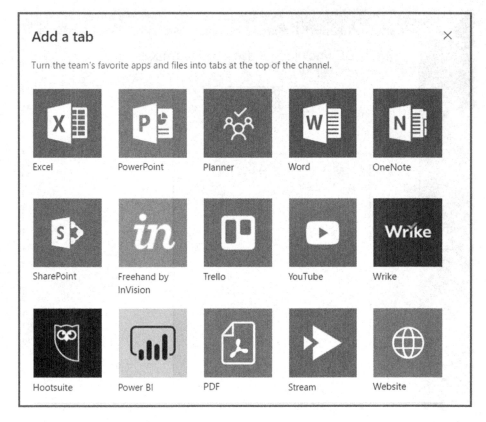

Figure 3-14. *Multiple custom tabs*

Custom Tab: Power BI

You can integrate a Power BI dashboard into a team channel. Follow these steps to integrate a PowerBI dashboard:

1. Select a team channel. Then, to the right of your existing tabs, select the plus (+) icon.

2. From the available list, select Power BI.

3. Name the new tab as you want, and then choose one of your Power BI workspaces from the drop-down menu.

4. Click the Save button.

Custom Tab: OneNote

OneNote is good for collaboration within a team. You can integrate OneNote into your channel by creating a OneNote tab. Add a tab for One Note via these steps:

1. Select a team channel where you want to add the tab.

2. To the right of your existing tabs, click the plus (+) icon.

3. Select the OneNote option.

4. Name your OneNote tab and then click Save.

Can you move an existing OneNote notebook into Teams?

If you have relevant content in another OneNote notebook, you can move it to the OneNote notebook associated with your team. Just open both notebooks in the desktop client and use the Merge feature.

BEST PRACTICES FOR ORGANIZING TEAMS IN MICROSOFT TEAMS

- Always think about the purpose of the team you are creating— for example, for a project or a task—and about who is going to be part of the team, to help deliver that goal collaboratively.

- Be selective when adding members to teams, so you can ensure that those members can help achieve your goal.

- It is a good idea to set up more than one owner for each team, in order to minimize dependency on a single owner.

- Use an existing Office 365 group, if available, to eliminate group duplication and potential confusion.

- Try to avoid creating different teams that have the same set of members, as this approach may not provide the desired focus you need to deliver the project or goal. Outlook is a great tool for sharing those types of group-wide communications.

- After creating teams, it is a good idea to start to think about the different areas of conversations that you want to have to work toward your goal. Thencreate initial channels so people know where to contribute and where to find existing conversations.

- Be descriptive when naming the channels, to make it easier for users to understand the goals of the conversations in the channel. You can add new tabs to channels to add tools such as OneNote, PowerBI, or links to web pages and other content. Those tabs can make it easy for people to find content and share it.

- Always utilize the General channel, which is created by default for you when you create the team. You can use General channel to share an overview of what the team wants to achieve and other high-level information that a new team member would find useful.

- You cannot remove or unfavorite the General channel, so use it to pin the project charter or welcome deck. This will ensure that as new people join your team, they'll have a single source of truth for your objectives.

- While naming channels, always remember that the channels will be ordered alphabetically after the General channel.

Managing and Controlling Teams via Custom Policies

Using policies to manage teams is always helpful in customizing the user experience. Policies can play an important role in customizing teams, because one size does not fit all, the same way single team settings cannot fit all teams.

So far, Microsoft Teams has limited policies. Going forward, Microsoft will publish more Teams-specific policies to tailor the Teams experience for users. If you are using Skype for Business as your unified communication and collaboration product, your life is easy; Teams will honor existing Skype for Business Online PSTN Conferencing & Calling Plans per-user setting polices.

Microsoft is going to release more user-level policies and Team-specific policies to support full customization with all exposed settings. Available policies right now are CsTeamsInteropPolicy, CsTeamsMeetingPolicy, and CsTeamsCallingPolicy.

Managing Guest Access

In Microsoft Teams, guest access enables an organization to collaborate with external partners. For example, you can allow other companies access to your teams and channels, including conversations, calls/meetings, and files, while maintaining granular control. As a team owner, you can invite partners or customers who have Azure Active Directory tenant accounts (e-mail address) or any consumer account (e-mail address). Previously, guest access was allowed only for Azure Active Directory tenant accounts. However, recently Microsoft announced guest access for consumer accounts as well. Teams guest access relies on the Azure Active Directory business-to-business platform, which allows directory-based authentication.

Understanding Subscription Requirements

You might be wondering whether you need an extra Office 365 subscription plan for guest access. No, you don't. Guest access is included with all Office 365 Business Premium, Office 365 Enterprise, and Office 365 Education subscriptions. No additional Office 365 license is necessary. Guest access is a tenant-level setting in Microsoft Teams and is turned off by default.

As an IT administrator, you can easily control guest access in your organization. For example, you can decide who can invite a guest into teams as well as what type of domain guest can be invited. A team owner or member can invite a guest to access the team; however, as an administrator, you can control this experience by using Azure Active Directory external access.

Microsoft Teams relies on the Office 365 group and the Azure Active Directory business-to-business platform. After you add any external user as a guest to Teams, in the back end IT manages Teams actually provisions the guest user in Azure Active Directory.

Table 3-1 compares the Microsoft Teams functionality available for an organization's team members to the functionality available for a guest user on the team.

Table 3-1.   *Team User and Guest Capabilities*

Capability in Teams	Teams user in the organization	Guest user
Create a channel (Team owners control this setting.)	Yes	Yes
Participate in a private chat	Yes	Yes
Participate in a channel conversation	Yes	Yes
Post, delete, and edit messages	Yes	Yes
Share a channel file	Yes	Yes
Share a chat file	Yes	No
Add apps (tabs, bots, or connectors)	Yes	No
Create tenant-wide and teams/channels guest access policies	Yes	No
Invite a user outside the Office 365 tenant's domain (Team owners control this setting)	Yes	No
Create a team	Yes	No
Discover and join a public team	Yes	No
View organization chart	Yes	No

Enabling Guest Access in Teams

To enable guest access in Teams, you first have to log on to the Office 365 portal (`https://portal.office.com/adminportal/home`. When theAdmin Center opens, choose Settings ➤ Services & Add-ins, as shown in Figure 3-15. Then find Microsoft Teams and click it.

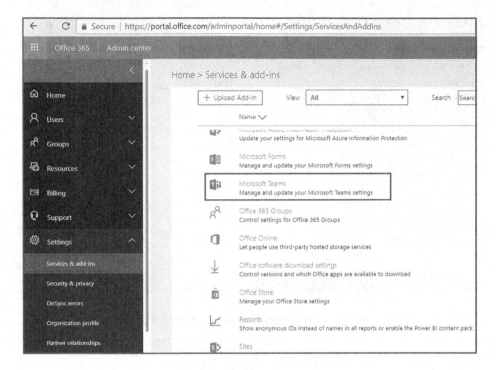

Figure 3-15. *Microsoft Teams in services*

From the Microsoft Teams page, open the Tenant-wide Settings. Under the Settings by User/License Type option, select the user/license type you want to configure. For this example, select Guest and then click Save, as shown in Figure 3-16.

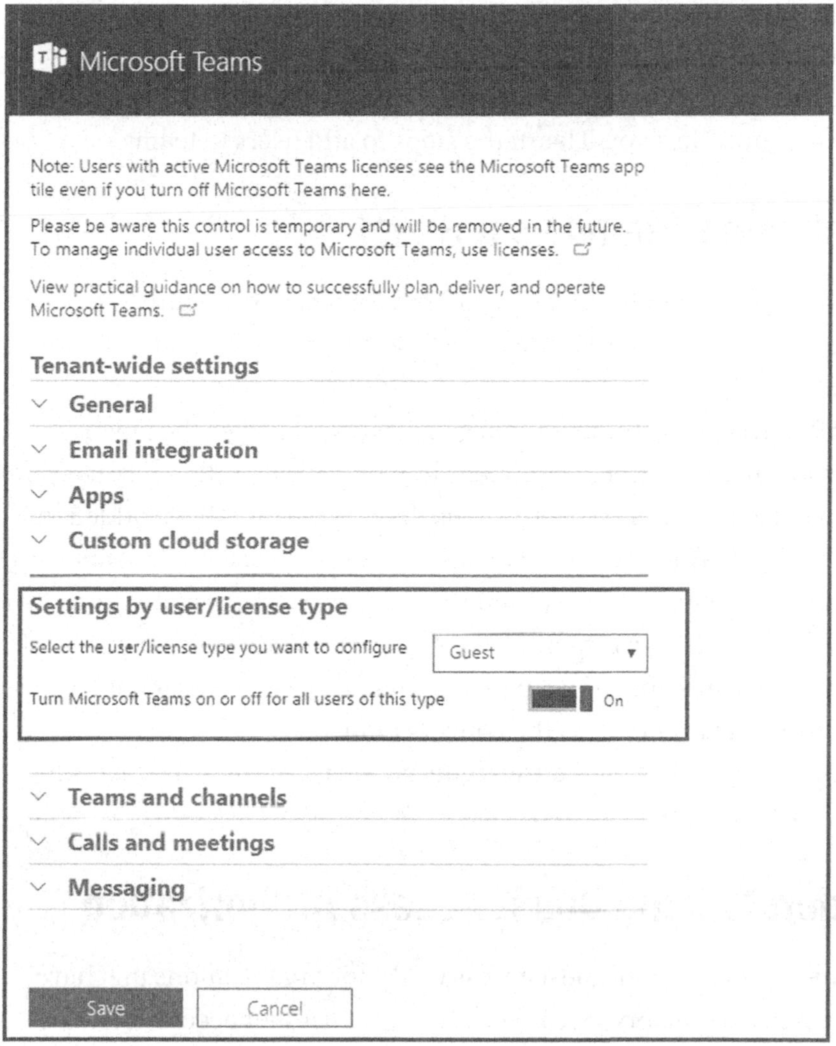

Figure 3-16. *Enabling guest access*

After you click Save, enabling guest access takes some time. Along with
Teams guest access, you also want to enable guest/external access in Azure
Active Directory, Office 365 groups, SharePoint, and OneDrive for Business
to fully utilize guest access functionality. Refer to the "Enabling External
Access in Azure AD" and "Enabling Guest Access in an Office 365 Group"
sections later in this chapter.

Enabling guest access will allow a team owner or member to invite guests to your team. Guest access is a tenant-wide setting.

Once guest access is activated, you can invite external users as guests to your teams. Next you'll learn the steps to add users to teams.

Accessing Teams as a Guest

When a team owner (or member) invites a guest to the team, that person will receive an e-mail indicating that "<so and so> added you as a guest to teams ...."

After accepting the invitation, guest users then click the Open Microsoft Teams button. That opens th eAzure Active Directory consent page, which provides access to teams that the user has been added to.

Another way to accept a team invitation is for a user to first open Teams. The user's picture will show which teams that user has been invited to. Once the user accepts, the Azure Active Directory consent page will switch the Teams app from a base tenant to a guest access tenant, where the guest can participate in the conversation.

Guest access has boundaries; guests can access only the teams to which they have been invited.

Understanding Guest Access Authorization

As I mentioned earlier, guest access works for organizations that have Azure Active Directory (AAD) accounts or consumer accounts such as those at yahoo.com and gmail.com. Also, there is great control available at the tenant level. All the authorization levels apply to your Office 365 tenant. Each authorization level controls the guest experience as shown here:

- *Azure Active Directory*: Guest access in Microsoft Teams relies on the Azure AD business-to-business (B2B) platform. Controls the guest experience at the directory, tenant, and application level.

- *Microsoft Teams*: Controls Microsoft Teams only.

- *Office 365 Groups*: Controls the guest experience in Office 365 Groups and Microsoft Teams.

- *SharePoint Online and OneDrive for Business*: Controls the guest experience in SharePoint Online, OneDrive for Business, Office 365 Groups, and Microsoft Teams.

As showed in Figure 3-17, Accessing authorization Teams.

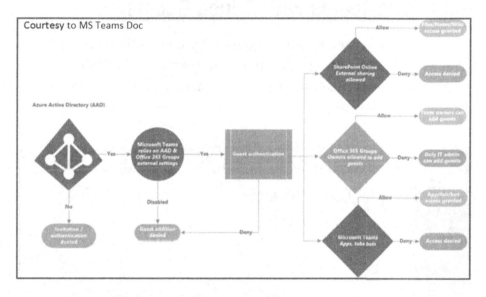

Figure 3-17. *Accessing authorization Teams*

If the entered guest account (e-mail address) is not from Azure Active Directory, the invitation or authentication will be denied. If the invited guest account address is from Azure AD, it goes to Microsoft Teams, because Teams relies on Azure AD and Office 365 Groups external settings. If external access is denied, the guest authentication gets denied as well. If external access is allowed, the guest gets authenticated and can then use the rest of the features that are dependent on SharePoint Online external sharing and Office 365 group owners allowed settings.

Guest access to SharePoint online is dependent on whether your tenant setting is set to allow access to Office 365 applications.

For example, if SharePoint access is not allowed for an external user, you can still invite that guest user to your teams. However, that guest will not be able to access files in Teams. Remember, Teams files are available through SharePoint Online. Guest access is based on the workload level and external access level.

Identifying Teams with Added Guests

When you add an external user as a guest to your team, that team will have a This Team Has Guests tag added under the team's name, as shown in Figure 3-18. The tag enables you, as a team member, to easily see that this team has guest users added.

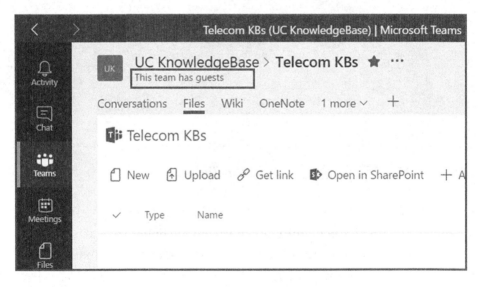

Figure 3-18. *A guest tag has been added to the team*

Another indicator alerts you that a guest has been added. When you view the team member list, you will now see a banner stating, "This team contains users from outside your organization" (see Figure 3-19).

Figure 3-19. *The team includes a guest*

Also, you can see a list of team members and their roles, and the guest user role will be labeled *Guest*.

Enabling External Access in Azure AD

There is another important setting in Azure AD where you can control guest access.

1. Log on to Office 365 Admin Center.

2. Then click Admin Center and then click Azure AD.

3. In Azure Active Directory admin center then click Azure Active Directory.

4. Click on User Settings.

5. Under External users, enable option as show in Figure 3-20.

Note that all these settings are enabled by default (set to yes).

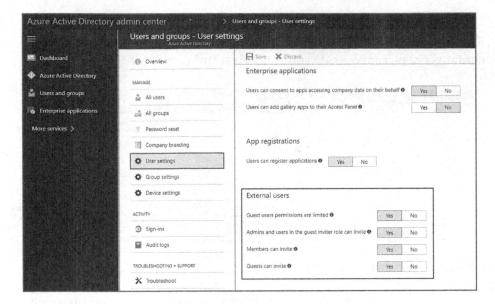

Figure 3-20.   External access in Azure AD

External Users' Settings

Four options are available to allow or disallow external users, and each option has different uses. Here are the details for each option:

- *Guest users permissions are limited*:

  - Yes—Guests do not have permission for certain directory tasks, such as enumerating users, groups, or other directory resources. Guests cannot be assigned to administrative roles in your directory.

  - No—Guests have the same access to directory data that regular users have in your directory.

- *Admins and users in the guest inviter role can invite*:

  - Yes—Admins and users in the Guest Inviter role will be able to invite guests to the tenant.

  - No—They will not be able to invite.

- *Members can invite*:

    - Yes—Non-admin members of your directory can invite guests to collaborate on resources secured by your Azure AD, such as SharePoint sites or Azure resources.

    - No—Only administrators can invite guests to your directory.

- *Guests can invite*:

    - Yes—Guests in your directory can themselves invite other guests to collaborate on resources secured by your Azure AD, such as SharePoint sites or Azure resources.

    - No—Guests cannot invite other guests to collaborate with your organization.

Enabling Guest Access in an Office 365 Group

Apart from Azure Active Directory external user access, another tenant-level control is available for IT administrator: the Office 365 group. Using Office 365 groups, you can control adding guest users and guest access to all Office 365 groups and Microsoft Teams in your organization. This is again a tenant-wide setting available for IT admins.

1. Log on to the Office 365 portal (`https://portal.office.com/adminportal/home`) by using a global admin account.

2. After the Admin Center opens, from the navigation menu choose Settings ➤ Services & Add-ins.

3. Select the Office 365 Groups option.

4. On the Office 365 Groups page, set the toggle
   to on next to "Let group members outside the
   organization access group content," as shown in
   Figure 3-21. If you turn this off, guests will still be
   listed as members of the group, but they won't
   receive group e-mails or be able to access any group
   content. They'll be able to access only individual
   group files that were directly shared with them.

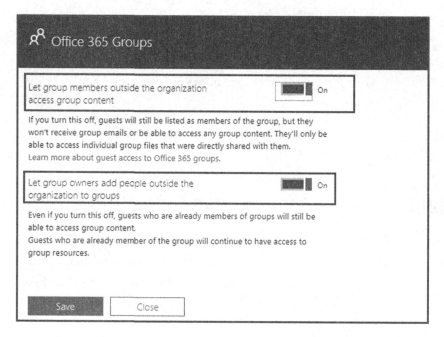

Figure 3-21. *Enabling guest access for Office 365 groups*

I recommend turning on this option, because it enables your
organization's users to add guest partners to their teams and channels for
the purpose of communication.

Next, you will see another option to control whether you want to let group and team owners add people outside your organization to Office 365 groups and Microsoft Teams. Set this toggle to on if you want to let group and team owners add guest users.

If you turn off "Let group owners add people outside the organization to groups," guests who are already members of groups will still be able to access group content. Guests who are already members of the group will continue to have access to group resources.

The preceding settings apply at the tenant level and control the guest experience in Office 365 groups and Microsoft Teams.

Using Team-Owner-Specific Control

An individual team-specific control is also available for guest access. The team owner has granular control over their team.

To modify this team access control setting, you must be the team owner. Here are the steps:

1. Select the specific teams for which you want to modify the access setting.

2. Select the ellipsis (...) to the right of the team name.

3. to View teams ➤ Then click the Manage Team option, as shown in Figure 3-22.

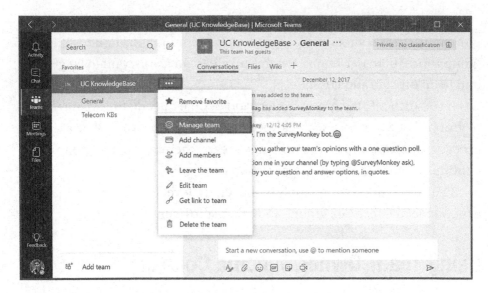

Figure 3-22. *Managing a team*

After the Manage Team window opens, click the Settings tab and then expand Guest Permissions to see the control settings available, as shown in Figure 3-23.

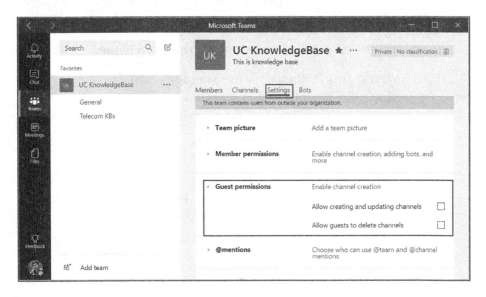

Figure 3-23. *Guest permissions*

Customize the guest access permissions at the team level. When you change the following settings, they will apply only to the current team where you are modifying the setting:

- *Allow creating and updating channels*: When you select this check box, you are allowing your guest to create and update the channel. I recommend not allowing this for all guests.

- *Allow guests to delete channels*: When you select this check box, you are allowing your guest to delete channels. I recommend not allowing this for all guests, because they could delete the entire channel.

Using PowerShell to Manage the Teams Experience

Microsoft provides multiple PowerShell commands that you can use for administration and management of your Microsoft teams. By using PowerShell commands, you can perform the following tasks:

- Create and modify teams

- Create and modify channels

- Add or remove team members

- Add or remove the team owner

- Set the team's guest setting

- Set teams and the team picture

Note   The PowerShell cmdlets are currently in Beta.

Figure 3-24 shows a list of PowerShell commands available for teams.

```
PS C:\> Get-TeamHelp

cmdlets
------------------------------
Get-TeamHelp
Connect-MicrosoftTeams
Disconnect-MicrosoftTeams
Get-Team
Get-TeamUser
Get-TeamChannel
Get-TeamMemberSettings
Get-TeamMessagingSettings
Get-TeamFunSettings
Get-TeamGuestSettings
New-Team
New-TeamChannel
Add-TeamUser
Remove-Team
Remove-TeamChannel
Remove-TeamUser
Set-TeamMemberSettings
Set-TeamMessagingSettings
Set-TeamFunSettings
Set-TeamGuestSettings
Set-TeamPicture
Set-Team
Set-TeamChannel

PS C:\>
```

Figure 3-24. *List of PowerShell commands for teams*

Connect to Microsoft Teams PowerShell

You can save the Microsoft Teams PowerShell module configuration file to a specified location. Here is the syntax:

```
Save-Module -Name MicrosoftTeams -Path "C:\temp\"
```

Next, type Y, as shown in Figure 3-25, to install NuGet.

```
PS C:\> Save-Module -Name MicrosoftTeams -Path "c:\temp\MicrosoftTeams"

NuGet provider is required to continue
PowerShellGet requires NuGet provider version '2.8.5.201' or newer to interact with NuGet-based repositories. The NuGet
 provider must be available in 'C:\Program Files\PackageManagement\ProviderAssemblies' or
'C:\Users\bilag\AppData\Local\PackageManagement\ProviderAssemblies'. You can also install the NuGet provider by running
 'Install-PackageProvider -Name NuGet -MinimumVersion 2.8.5.201 -Force'. Do you want PowerShellGet to install and
import the NuGet provider now?
[Y] Yes  [N] No  [S] Suspend  [?] Help (default is "Y"): y
```

Figure 3-25. *Installing NuGet*

You can directly install the Microsoft Teams module by using this command:

```
Install-Module -Name MicrosoftTeams
```

You'll get a warning message indicating, "You are installing the modules from an untrusted repository." Press Y to install Teams, as shown in Figure 3-26.

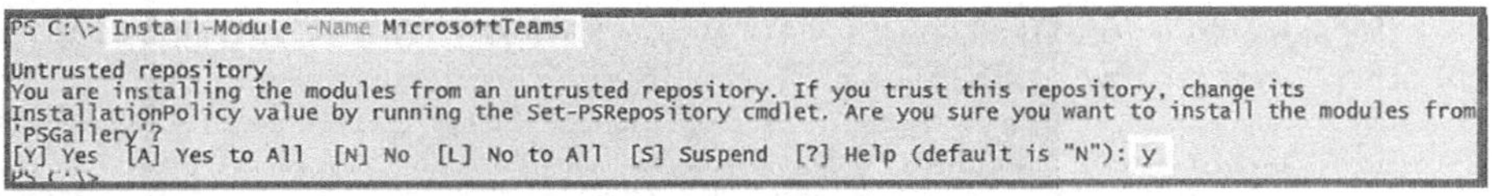

```
PS C:\> Install-Module -Name MicrosoftTeams

Untrusted repository
You are installing the modules from an untrusted repository. If you trust this repository, change its
InstallationPolicy value by running the Set-PSRepository cmdlet. Are you sure you want to install the modules from
'PSGallery'?
[Y] Yes  [A] Yes to All  [N] No  [L] No to All  [S] Suspend  [?] Help (default is "N"): y
PS C:\>
```

Figure 3-26. *Installing the Teams PowerShell module*

Now that the Teams module is installed, it's time to import the Microsoft Teams module via PowerShell:

```
PS C:\>Import-Module MicrosoftTeams
PS C:\> $cred = Get-Credential
```

As showed in Figure 3-27, Enter credential to access Team setting using PowerShell.

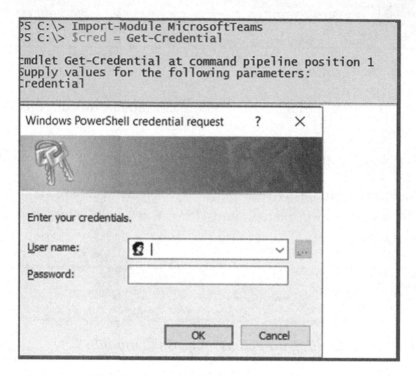

Figure 3-27. *Login windows*

Supply values for the credentials which as Office 365 Tenant Admin permission.

Then Run this command to connect Microsoft teams:

```
Connect-MicrosoftTeams -Credential $cred
```

Because you already stored the Office 365 tenant credential in $cred, you can connect to Microsoft Teams. You can use the PowerShell commands shown in Figure 3-28.

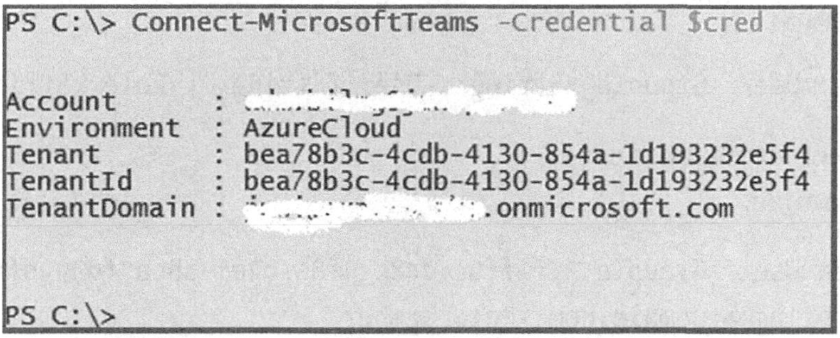

```
PS C:\> Connect-MicrosoftTeams -Credential $cred

Account        :
Environment    : AzureCloud
Tenant         : bea78b3c-4cdb-4130-854a-1d193232e5f4
TenantId       : bea78b3c-4cdb-4130-854a-1d193232e5f4
TenantDomain   :                    .onmicrosoft.com


PS C:\>
```

Figure 3-28. Connecting Microsoft Teams

Note   Currently, most of these PowerShell commands are in Beta.

Add-TeamUser

You can use the Add-TeamUser command to add an owner or members to teams.

The result will show immediately; however, it takes some time before changes are reflected. To turn an existing member into an owner, you first add the person to the owner's list:

```
Add-TeamUser -Role Owner -User Bilag
```

Then you to remove that person from the members list:

```
Remove-TeamUser -User Bilag
```

Syntax:

```
Add-TeamUser -GroupId <String> -User <String> [-Role <String>]
```

Role: Member or Owner

Example:

```
Add-TeamUser -GroupId 31f1ff6c-d48c-4f8a-b2e1-abca7fd399df
-User bilag@mydomain.com -Role Member
```

```
PS C:\> Add-TeamUser -GroupId ba092401-2eca-4a84-ab5c-f70654c37344 -User pjoaquim@            -Role Member
PS C:\>
```

So how do you get a group ID for your team?

Run this command with your team's name:

```
$team = Get-Team | ? {$_.DisplayName -eq "Yourteamname"}
$team.GroupId
```

Disconnect-MicrosoftTeams

This cmdlet is in Beta.

Syntax:

```
Disconnect-MicrosoftTeams [-WhatIf] [-Confirm]
```

Get-Team

This command lists all the teams that the user is part of. The user must be you. (You can get only information on yourself. Keep in mind that Office 365 administrators can't use Get-Team to get team information across organizations unless they are a member of all teams.)

Syntax:

```
Get-Team [-User <String>]
```

Example:

```
Get-Team -User bilag@mydomain.com
```

If the user running this PowerShell command doesn't have a Teams license assigned, that user cannot run this command; see Figure 3-29. First assign the license and then run the same command.

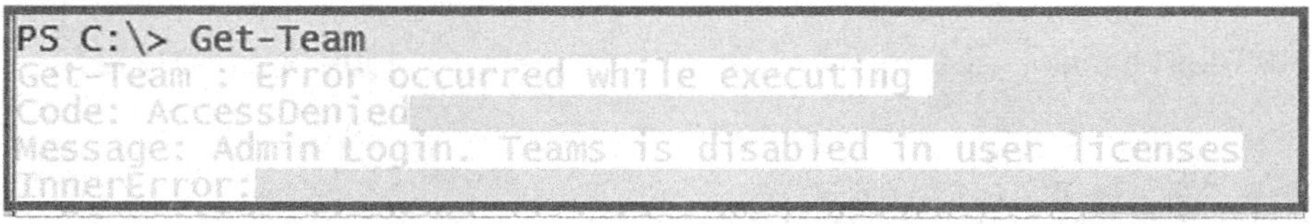

```
PS C:\> Get-Team
Get-Team : Error occurred while executing
Code: AccessDenied
Message: Admin Login. Teams is disabled in user licenses
InnerError:
```

Figure 3-29. *Error: access denied*

In my case, I assigned a Microsoft Teams license to my account, and then waited 4–5 minutes for the changes to be reflected. Run the same command again and see the result, as shown in Figure 3-30.

```
PS C:\> Get-Team

GroupId                              DisplayName      Description
-------                              -----------      -----------
ba092401-2eca-4a84-ab5c-f70654c37344 UC KnowledgeBase This is knowledge base

PS C:\>
```

Figure 3-30. *Command result*

You cannot run the Get-Team command except from your account. Otherwise, you'll get the error shown in Figure 3-31.

```
PS C:\> Get-Team -User bilag@mydomain.com
Get-Team : Error occurred while executing
Code: InvalidRequest
Message: This request is supported in current user context only
InnerError:
```

Figure 3-31. *Command access error*

Get-TeamChannel

You can use this command to get all the channels for a team.

Syntax:

```
Get-TeamChannel  -GroupId <String>
```

Example:

```
Get-TeamChannel -GroupId af55e84c-dc67-4e48-9005-86e0b07272f9
```

Get-TeamFunSettings

This command gets a team's function settings.

Syntax:

```
Get-TeamFunSettings -GroupId <String>
```

Example:

```
Get-TeamFunSettings -GroupId 2f162b0e-36d2-4e15-8ba3-
ba229cecdccf
```

Get-TeamGuestSettings

This command gets the team's guest settings.

Syntax:

```
Get-TeamGuestSettings -GroupId <String>
```

Example:

```
Get-TeamGuestSettings -GroupId 2f162b0e-36d2-4e15-8ba3-
ba229cecdccf
```

Get-TeamHelp

This command gets a list of all commands for Microsoft Teams.

Example:

```
Get-TeamHelp
```

Get-TeamMemberSettings

You use this command to gets team member settings.

Syntax:

```
Get-TeamMemberSettings -GroupId <String>
```

Example:

```
Get-TeamMemberSettings -GroupId 2f162b0e-36d2-4e15-8ba3-
ba229cecdccf
```

Get-TeamMessagingSettings

This command gets team messaging settings.

Syntax:

```
Get-TeamMessagingSettings -GroupId <String>
```

Example:

```
Get-TeamMessagingSettings -GroupId 2f162b0e-36d2-4e15-8ba3-
ba229cecdccf
```

Get-TeamUser

Use this command to see the users of a team.

Syntax:

```
Get-TeamUser -GroupId <String> [-Role <String>]
```

Example:

```
Get-TeamUser -GroupId 2f162b0e-36d2-4e15-8ba3-ba229cecdccf
-Role Owner
```

New-Team

This command creates a new team. The new team will be backed by a new unified group. The command creates a new team with user-specified settings, and returns a Group object with a GroupID property.

Syntax:

```
New-Team -DisplayName <String> [-Description <String>] [-Alias
<String>] [-Classification <String>] [-AccessType <String>]
[-AddCreatorAsMember <Boolean>]
```

Example:

```
New-Team -DisplayName "Tech Reads"
New-Team -DisplayName "Tech Reads" -Description "Team to post
technical articles and blogs" -AccessType Public
Connect-MicrosoftTeams -AccountId bilag@mydomain.com
$group = New-Team -alias "TestTeam" -displayname "Test Teams"
-AccessType "private"
Add-TeamUser -GroupId $group.GroupId -User "fred@example.com"
Add-TeamUser -GroupId $group.GroupId -User "john@example.com"
Add-TeamUser -GroupId $group.GroupId -User "wilma@example.com"
```

```
New-TeamChannel -GroupId $group.GroupId -DisplayName "Q4 planning"
New-TeamChannel -GroupId $group.GroupId -DisplayName "Exec status"
New-TeamChannel -GroupId $group.GroupId -DisplayName "Contracts"
Set-TeamFunSettings -GroupId $group.GroupId -AllowCustomMemes true

Get-MsolGroup -SearchString "TestyTest" | Where-Object
DisplayName -eq TestyTest | foreach-object -process {
        $name = "TestConvert" + $_.DisplayName
        $group = New-Team -displayname $name
        Get-MsolGroupMember -GroupObjectId $_.ObjectId |
        foreach-object -process {
                Add-TeamUser -GroupId $group.GroupId -User
                $_.EmailAddress
        }
}
```

New-TeamChannel

This command adds a new channel to a team.

Syntax:

```
New-TeamChannel
-GroupId <String> -DisplayName <String> [-Description <String>]
```

Example:

```
New-TeamChannel -GroupId 126b90a5-e65a-4fef-98e3-d9b49f4acf12
-DisplayName "Architecture"
```

Note   The channel display name (DisplayName) must be 50 characters or fewer, and can't contain these characters # % & * { } / \ : < > ? | ' ". The channel description can be up to 1,024 characters.

Remove-Team

This command will allow you to delete a team.

Syntax:

```
Remove-Team -GroupId <String>
```

Example:

```
Remove-Team -GroupId 31f1ff6c-d48c-4f8a-b2e1-abca7fd399df
```

Remove-TeamChannel

This cmdlet will allow you to delete a channel.

Note   This command will not delete content in associated tabs.
In addition, the channel will be *soft deleted*, meaning the contents
are not permanently deleted for a time. A subsequent call to
Add-TeamChannel using the same channel name will fail if enough
time has not passed.

Syntax:

```
Remove-TeamChannel -GroupId <String> -DisplayName <String>
```

Example:

```
Remove-TeamChannel -GroupId 2f162b0e-36d2-4e15-8ba3-
ba229cecdccf -DisplayName "Tech Reads"
```

- -DisplayName is the channel name to be deleted.

Remove-TeamUser

You can use this command to remove an owner or member from a team, and from the unified group that backs the team.

The command will return immediately, but the Teams application will not reflect the update immediately. The Teams application may need to be open for up to an hour before changes are reflected there.

The last owner cannot be removed from the team.

To turn an existing member into an owner, first add the person as an owner:

```
Add-TeamUser -Role Owner -User foo
```

Then remove that person from the members list:

```
Remove-TeamUser -User foo
```

Syntax:

```
Remove-TeamUser
-GroupId <String> -User <String>
```

Example:

```
Remove-TeamUser -GroupId 31f1ff6c-d48c-4f8a-b2e1-abca7fd399df
-User bilag@mydomain.com
```

Set-Team

This command updates a team and its settings.

Syntax:

```
Set-Team
-GroupId <String> [-DisplayName <String>] [-Description <String>]
[-Alias <String>] [-Classification <String>] [-AccessType <String>]
```

Example:

```
Set-Team -GroupId 2f162b0e-36d2-4e15-8ba3-ba229cecdccf
-DisplayName "Updated TeamName" -AccessType Public
```

- -AccessType: Team access type. Valid values are Private and Public.

- -Alias: Same as DisplayName without any spaces; limited to 64 characters

- -Classification: Team classification.

- -DisplayName: Team display name; limited to 256 characters.

- -Description: Team description; limited to 1,024 characters.

Set-TeamChannel

This command updates the team's channel settings.

Syntax:

```
Set-TeamChannel -GroupId <String> -CurrentDisplayName <String>
[-NewDisplayName <String>] [-Description <String>]
```

Example:

```
Set-TeamChannel -GroupId c58566a6-4bb4-4221-98d4-47677dbdbef6
-CurrentDisplayName TechReads -NewDisplayName "Technical Reads"
Set-TeamChannel -GroupId c58566a6-4bb4-4221-98d4-47677dbdbef6
-CurrentDisplayName TechReads -NewDisplayName "Technical Reads"
```

- -NewDisplayName: New channel display name. Names must be 50 characters or fewer, and can't contain the characters # % & * { } / \ : < > ? | ' ".

- -Description: Updated channel description; limited to 1,024 characters.

Remove-TeamUser

This cmdlet is currently in Beta. The cmdlet removes an owner or member from a team, and from the unified group that backs the team.

The command will return immediately, but the Teams application will not reflect the update immediately. The Teams application may need to be open for up to an hour before changes are reflected.

The last owner cannot be removed from the team.

To turn an existing member into an owner, first add the person as an owner:

```
Add-TeamUser -Role Owner -User foo
```

Then remove the person from the members list:

```
Remove-TeamUser -User foo
```

Syntax:

```
Remove-TeamUser -GroupId <String> -User <String>
```

Example:

```
Remove-TeamUser -GroupId 31f1ff6c-d48c-4f8a-b2e1-abca7fd399df
-User dmx@example.com
```

Set-Team

This command updates a team.

Syntax:

```
Set-Team -GroupId <String> [-DisplayName <String>]
[-Description <String>]
[-Alias <String>] [-Classification <String>] [-AccessType
<String>]
```

Example:

```
Set-Team -GroupId 2f162b0e-36d2-4e15-8ba3-ba229cecdccf
-DisplayName "Updated TeamName" -AccessType Public
```

- -GroupId: GroupId of the team.

- -AccessType: Team access type. Valid values are Private and Public.

- -Alias: Same as DisplayName without any spaces; limited to 64 characters.

- -Classification: Team classification.

- -Description: Team description; limited to 1,024 characters.

- -DisplayName: Team display name; limited to 256 characters.

Set-TeamChannel

This command updates the team's channel settings.

Syntax:

```
Set-TeamChannel -GroupId <String> -CurrentDisplayName <String>
[-NewDisplayName <String>] [-Description <String>]
```

Example:

```
Set-TeamChannel -GroupId c58566a6-4bb4-4221-98d4-47677dbdbef6
-CurrentDisplayName TechReads -NewDisplayName "Technical Reads"
```

- -CurrentDisplayName: Current channel name.

- -GroupId: Group ID of the team.

- `-Description`: Updated channel description; limited to 1,024 characters.

- `-NewDisplayName`: New channel display name. Names must be 50 characters or fewer, and can't contain the characters # % & * { } / \ : < > ?.

Set-TeamFunSettings

This command updates Giphy, sticker, and meme settings.

Syntax:

```
Set-TeamFunSettings -GroupId <String> [-AllowGiphy <String>]
[-GiphyContentRating <String>] [-AllowStickersAndMemes <String>]
[-AllowCustomMemes <String>]
```

Example:

```
Set-TeamFunSettings -GroupId 0ebb500c-f5f3-44dd-b155-
cc8c4f383e2d -AllowGiphy true -GiphyContentRating Strict
```

- `-GroupId`: Group ID of the team.

- `-AllowCustomMemes`: Allows custom memes to be uploaded.

- `-AllowGiphy`: Enables Giphy file for the team.

- `-AllowStickersAndMemes`: Enables stickers and memes.

- `-GiphyContentRating`: Sets content rating for Giphy file. Can be `Strict` or `Moderate`.

Set-TeamGuestSettings

This command updates team guest settings.

Syntax:

```
Set-TeamGuestSettings -GroupId <String>
[-AllowCreateUpdateChannels <String>] [-AllowDeleteChannels <String>]
```

Example:

```
Set-TeamGuestSettings -GroupId a61f5a96-a0cf-43db-a7c8-
cec05f8a8fc4 -AllowCreateUpdateChannels true
```

- -GroupId: Group ID of the team.

- -AllowCreateUpdateChannels: Settings to create and update channels.

- -AllowDeleteChannels: Settings to delete channels.

Set-TeamMemberSettings:

This command updates team member settings.

Syntax:

```
Set-TeamMemberSettings -GroupId <String>
[-AllowCreateUpdateChannels <String>]
[-AllowDeleteChannels <String>] [-AllowAddRemoveApps
<String>] [-AllowCreateUpdateRemoveTabs <String>]
[-AllowCreateUpdateRemoveConnectors <String>]
```

Example:

```
Set-TeamMemberSettings -GroupId 4ba546e6-e28d-4645-8cc1-
d3575ef9d266 -AllowCreateUpdateChannels false
```

```
Set-TeamMemberSettings -GroupId 4ba546e6-e28d-4645-8cc1-
d3575ef9d266 -AllowDeleteChannels true -AllowAddRemoveApps false
```

- -GroupId: Group ID of the team.

- -AllowAddRemoveApps: Setting to add and remove apps to/from teams.

- -AllowCreateUpdateChannels: Setting to create and update channels.

- -AllowCreateUpdateRemoveConnectors: Setting to create, update, and remove connectors.

- -AllowCreateUpdateRemoveTabs: Setting to create, update, and remove tabs.

- -AllowDeleteChannels: Setting to delete channels.

Set-TeamMessagingSettings:

This command updates team messaging settings.

Syntax:

```
Set-TeamMessagingSettings -GroupId <String>
[-AllowUserEditMessages <String>] [-AllowUserDeleteMessages
<String>] [-AllowOwnerDeleteMessages <String>]
[-AllowTeamMentions <String>] [-AllowChannelMentions <String>]
```

Example:

```
Set-TeamMessagingSettings -GroupId 4ba546e6-e28d-4645-8cc1-
d3575ef9d266 -AllowUserEditMessages true
Set-TeamMessagingSettings -GroupId 4ba546e6-e28d-
4645-8cc1-d3575ef9d266 -AllowUserDeleteMessages false
-AllowChannelMentions true
```

- `-GroupId`: Group ID of the team.

- `-AllowChannelMentions`: Allows @channel or @[channel name] mentions. This will notify members who've favorited that channel.

- `-AllowOwnerDeleteMessages`: Allow owner to delete messages.

- `-AllowTeamMentions`: Allows @team or @[team name] mentions. This will notify everyone on the team.

- `-AllowUserDeleteMessages`: Allows user to delete messages.

- `-AllowUserEditMessages`: Allows user to edit messages.

Set-TeamPicture

This command updates the team picture.

The command will return immediately, but the Teams application will not reflect the update immediately. The Teams application may need to be open for up to an hour before changes are reflected.

Syntax:

```
Set-TeamPicture -GroupId <String> -ImagePath <String>
```

Example:

```
Set-TeamPicture -GroupId 2f162b0e-36d2-4e15-8ba3-ba229cecdccf
-ImagePath c:\Image\TeamPictire.png
```

```
PS C:\> Set-TeamPicture -GroupId "ba092401-2eca-4a84-ab5c-f70654c37344" -ImagePath "C:\Balu\screenshot\Teams\Teams_pic.j
pg"
```

- `-GroupId`: Group ID of the team

- `-ImagePath`: File path and image (.png, .gif, .jpg, or .jpeg)

Summary

IT administrators can provision and manage users in their teams. Teams and channels are distinct from each other. Microsoft teams are a collection of people, content, and tools surrounding different projects and jobs within an organization, whereas channels are dedicated sections within a team that keep conversations organized by specific topics, projects, and disciplines that work for that team. In addition to having team members from your organization, the team owner can invite external partners as guests of the team conversation. Currently, guest access works only for organizations that have Azure Active Directory (AAD) accounts. You can manage the team experience through Office 365 Admin Center as well as through PowerShell.

CHAPTER 4

Teams Capabilities and Enhancement

The goal of this chapter is to help you understand the many capabilities of Teams, including audio/video conferencing. This chapter covers the following topics:

1. Audio conferencing

2. A/V call setup and media flow

3. Teams connectors and customization

4. Built-in and custom tabs in Teams

5. Microsoft Teams for Education sector

Audio Conferencing

Teams is a chat-based workspace in Office 365 that includes the capability to host meetings (online meetings and audio conferences). Meeting in teams is all about gathering people remotely so they can have conversations about their work.

© Balu N Ilag 2018
B.N. Ilag, *Introducing Microsoft Teams*, https://doi.org/10.1007/978-1-4842-3567-6_4

Meeting in Teams can vary in scope, from a channel meeting to a private meeting. A private meeting is shared with a selective group of attendees but not with the channel. In contrast, a channel meeting is shared with the channel and is visible to all team members; it's considered an open meeting within the channel, so any team member can join.

Audio conferencing is another important feature of Teams; audio conferencing in Office 365 allows conference participants to join Teams meetings from any telephone, including mobile and landline devices, without Internet access. This allows users to join Teams meetings by using their phones (using traditional landline, PBX, or mobile devices) to dial in for the audio portion of the meeting. Audio conferencing in Office 365 is available for Skype for Business Online and Microsoft Teams, and it works the same way in both.

Currently, the existing Skype for Business Admin Center and remote PowerShell provide the administrative interfaces used to manage audio conferencing for both Teams and Skype for Business.

Audio conferencing in Teams is available for scheduled meetings, but a tenant-level setting has to be enabled to use the audio conferencing feature.

Once audio conferencing is enabled and set up, anyone who has the dial-in number and conference ID can join a Microsoft Teams meeting, unless the meeting organizer has locked the meeting. The meeting organizer also has the ability to "mute" meeting attendees if desired.

Each meeting has a set maximum length of time, which can vary depending on who is in the meeting and the type of authentication used to join the meeting. Table 4-1 outlines the details of meeting length.

Table 4-1. *Meeting length and End Time*

Meeting Attendees	Meeting End Time
Users have joined by using a Skype for Business or Microsoft Teams app or have dialed in to the meeting.	The meeting ends if there are no changes to the attendee list after 24 hours.
All users have dialed in to the meeting, but someone has used a PIN to enter the meeting.	The meeting ends after 24 hours.
All users have dialed in to the meeting, and no one used a PIN to enter the meeting.	The meeting ends after 4 hours.

Each audio conferencing session allows up to 250 phone attendees. Audio conferencing users cannot get personal conference IDs. In Skype for Business and Microsoft Teams, users will be randomly assigned conferencing IDs and can't reserve or set a static conference ID that only they can use.

Various commands are used for in-meeting dial-pads; for example, press *6 to mute/unmute themselves, and press *1 to play the descriptions of available dial-pad commands.

Conference attendees can dial-out international phone numbers to invite other callers into a Skype for Business or Microsoft Teams meeting. Audio conferencing is the same for both Skype for Business and Microsoft Teams.

Understanding the Need for Audio Conferencing

Participants can use audio/video conferencing via a computer or mobile device, using a Voice over Internet Protocol (VoIP) network. However, limitations exist; for example, when a data network is not available or participants are not in front of a computer, or when Internet data connections are unavailable or unreliable to support voice communications. Unreliable connections may occur, for instance, when users are in a remote area with spotty mobile data coverage, or are connected to a free, public Wi-Fi service with limited bandwidth. The audio (dial-in) conference therefore plays an important role in providing an alternate way to join the audio portion of a conference call.

Meeting Licensing Requirements

An Audio Conferencing license, formerly known as a Skype for Business PSTN Conferencing license, is available as part of Office 365 E5 subscription plans, or as an add-on to Office 365 E1 or Office 365 E3 subscription plans.

Note   PSTN, or dial-in, conferencing in Teams does not support third-party audio conferencing providers (ACPs). Organizations that already use Skype for Business Online PSTN conferencing today can immediately take advantage of audio conferencing in Teams.

To provide toll-free conference bridge phone numbers and to support conferencing dial-out to international phone numbers, an organization must set up communications credits.

Follow these steps to assign an Audio Conferencing license:

1. Log on to the Office 365 portal with your work or school account. Choose Admin ➤ Users ➤ Active Users. Find your user and click Edit next to the product license.

2. In the list of licenses, choose Audio Conferencing and toggle the option to turn it on, as shown in Figure 4-1.

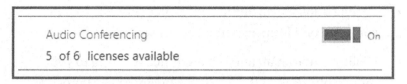

Figure 4-1. Audio Conferencing license

Understanding Communications Credits

Communications credits are a prepaid amounts of credit that will be available when required. Providing a toll-free conference bridge number and supporting dial-out to international phone numbers costs money. Allowing users to pay for these services with communications credits is recommended.

To set up and use a toll-free conference bridge number and provide the ability to dial-out to international numbers, you need to set up communications credits. This is also known as PSTN conferencing consumption billing.

Microsoft recommends having communications credits for Calling Plan and Audio Conferencing options, to give users the ability to dial out to any PSTN destination. Many countries/regions are included, but some destinations may not be included in your Calling Plan or Audio Conferencing subscriptions. If you don't set up communications credits or assign a license to your users, and you run out of minutes for your organization (depending on your Calling Plan, Audio Conferencing plan, or your country/region), those users won't be able to make calls or dial out from online audio conferencing meetings.

Having communications credits carries many advantages:

- Adding toll-free numbers to use with audio conferencing meetings, auto attendants, or call queues. Toll-free calls are billed per minute and require a positive communications credits balance.

153

- Dialing out from an audio conference meeting to add someone else from anywhere in the world.

- Dialing out from an audio conference meeting to your mobile phone with the Skype for Business or Microsoft Teams app installed to destinations that aren't already included in your subscription.

- Dialing any international phone number when you have Domestic Calling Plan subscriptions.

- Dialing international phone numbers beyond what is included in a Domestic and International Calling Plan subscription.

- Dialing out and paying per minute after you have exhausted your monthly minute allotment.

Setting Up Communications Credits

Organizations must set up communications credits and then assign a Communications Credits license for each user in the Office 365 Admin Center.

To set up communications credits, do the following:

1. Log on to the Office 365 portal and access the Office 365 Admin Center.

2. Choose Billing ➤ Subscriptions ➤ Add-ons ➤ Buy Add-ons. Then choose Communications Credits ➤ Buy Now.

3. On the Communications Credits subscription page, fill in your information and then click Next:

4. Add funds and set as Auto Recharge to avoid any disruption of service.

Once you've set up communications credits, you assign a license to the user:

1. In the Office 365 Admin Center, choose Users ➤ Active Users. Select a user or users from the list.

2. In the Action pane under Product licenses, click Edit.

3. On the Product licenses page, toggle Communications Credits to on to assign this license. Then click Save.

Setting Up Audio Conferencing

Note   Currently, Audio conferencing in Office 365 is not available in all countries. You can reference a list of available countries at `https://docs.microsoft.com/en-us/SkypeForBusiness/ country-and-region-availability-for-audio- conferencing-and-calling-plans/country-and-region- availability-for-audio-conferencing-and-calling- plans`. Before setting up audio conferencing, find out whether it is available in your region.

Audio conferencing has many advantages—for example, allowing users to join a Teams meeting when they are away from their desk or to join a meeting while driving or when a data network is not available. As I mentioned earlier, audio conferencing comes with Office 365 E5 or is available as an add-on for Office 365 E1 and E3. And having communications credits for a toll-free bridge number is recommended, because sometimes service will be interrupted if a bill is due or not processed in time.

155

Assuming these requirements are completed, let's start the configuration.

Note   Audio conferencing setup is required only for people who plan to schedule or lead meetings. Meeting attendees who dial in don't need any licenses assigned to them or other setup.

The following sections discuss what needs to be configured in audio conferencing (Microsoft bridge and Microsoft bridge settings).

Microsoft Bridge

Audio conferencing requires bridge number, follow the steps to choose bridge number:

1. Log on to Office 365 and then open the Office 365 Admin Center.

2. Choose Skype for Business ➤ Skype for Business Admin Center.

3. In the left navigation pane, choose Audio Conferencing ➤ Microsoft Bridge. Remember, I mentioned that audio conferencing is the same for Skype for Business and Microsoft Teams.

In the Microsoft Bridge tab, you can select dedicated and shared bridge numbers for your users to use. A shared number can be used by other tenants in Office 365, and a dedicated number can be used by your tenant only.

You can acquire a dedicated conference bridge number from Microsoft, or you can transfer or port your own conference numbers to Microsoft.

Figure 4-2 shows both dedicated and shared toll numbers. You can make any toll bridge number the default so that every time users schedule a conference, this number will show by default.

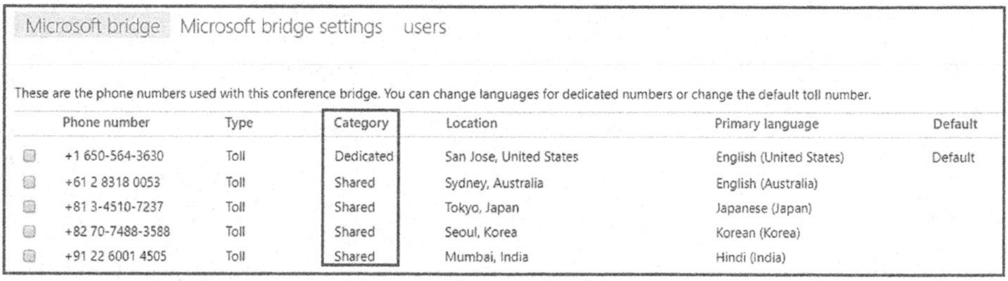

Phone number	Type	Category	Location	Primary language	Default
+1 650-564-3630	Toll	Dedicated	San Jose, United States	English (United States)	Default
+61 2 8318 0053	Toll	Shared	Sydney, Australia	English (Australia)	
+81 3-4510-7237	Toll	Shared	Tokyo, Japan	Japanese (Japan)	
+82 70-7488-3588	Toll	Shared	Seoul, Korea	Korean (Korea)	
+91 22 6001 4505	Toll	Shared	Mumbai, India	Hindi (India)	

Figure 4-2. *Toll bridge numbers*

Microsoft Bridge Settings

To change bridge setting, follow the below steps:

1. Log on to Office 365 with your work account. Then go to the Office 365 Admin Center.

2. Choose Skype for Business Admin Center. From the left navigation pane, choose Audio Conferencing ➤ Microsoft Bridge Settings.

3. On the Microsoft Bridge Settings page, select the options shown in Figure 4-3.

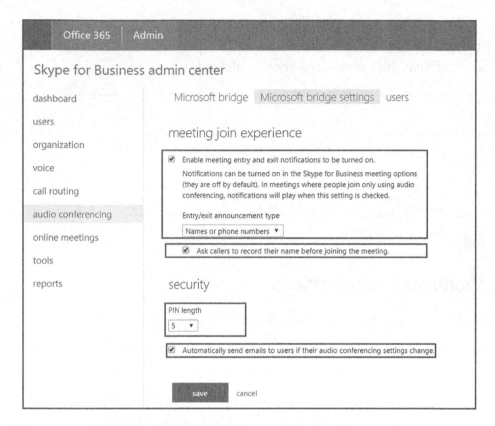

Figure 4-3. *Microsoft Bridge Settings options*

Details of these options are as follows:

- Under the Meeting Join Experience section, enable meeting entry and exit notifications to be turned on; this option is selected by default. If you clear the check box, users who have already joined the meeting won't be notified when someone enters or leaves the meeting.

- When you select Enable meeting entry and exit notifications to be turned on, you can select these options from the Entry/exit announcement type list:

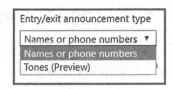

- *Names or phone numbers*: When users dial in to a meeting, their phone number will be played when they join it.

- *Tones (Preview)*: When users dial in to a meeting, an audio tone will be played when they join it.

Note   Using Tone as the announcement type is currently available to all customers as a preview feature.

- The check box to "Ask callers to record their name before joining the meeting" is selected by default. If you clear the check box, callers won't be asked to record their name before joining a meeting.

- In the Security section, set the PIN length by selecting the number of digits you want for the PIN in the PIN Length drop-down list.

- A PIN is required in order to join as an authenticated caller. The default PIN is 5 digits, but you can have a PIN from 4 to 12 digits. You can use this option to adjust audio conferencing security in order to match the security policy set up by your organization.

   If you select the check box labeled "Automatically send emails to users if their audio conference settings change," users will receive e-mail notification when audio conference settings are changed.

Click the Save button to save the changes.

Managing Audio Conference Settings

To manage audio conference settings, you must have Office 365 Admin
Control access. Follow these steps to manage audio conferencing settings:

1. Log on to Office 365 Portal and then choose Admin
   Centers ➤ Skype for Business.

2. In the Skype for Business Admin Center, Click on audio
   conferencing to see more settings as shown in Figure 4-4.

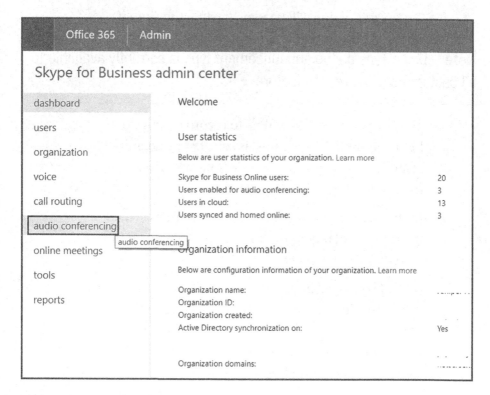

Figure 4-4. *Audio conferencing details*

3. Click the Users option. Select the user for whom
   you want to manage settings, and then in the Action
   pane, click Edit.

4. In the left navigation pane, choose Audio
   Conferencing. On the Properties page for the user to
   modify, as shown in Figure 4-5.

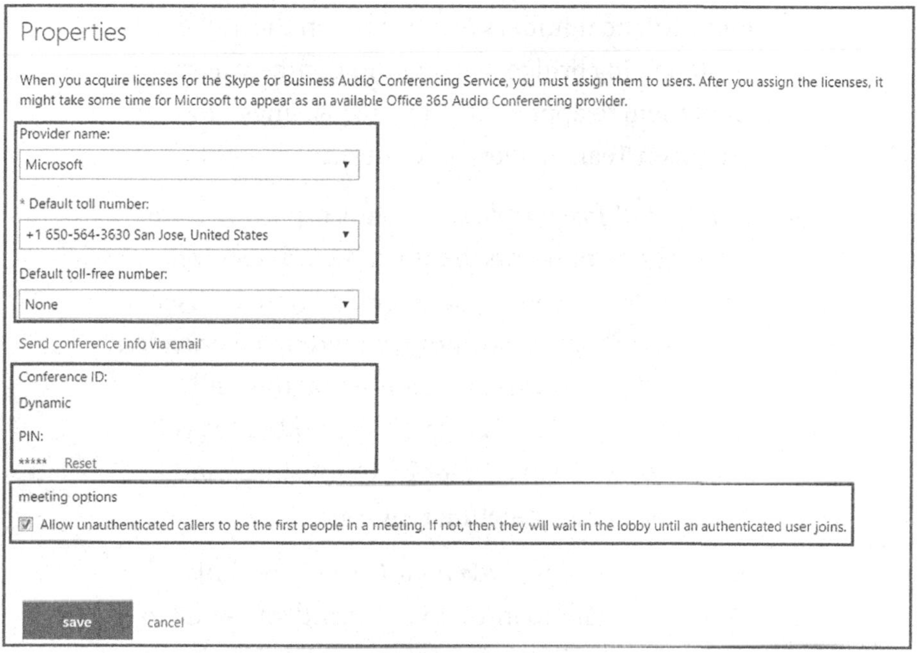

Properties

When you acquire licenses for the Skype for Business Audio Conferencing Service, you must assign them to users. After you assign the licenses, it might take some time for Microsoft to appear as an available Office 365 Audio Conferencing provider.

Provider name:

| Microsoft ▾ |

* Default toll number:

| +1 650-564-3630 San Jose, United States ▾ |

Default toll-free number:

| None ▾ |

Send conference info via email

Conference ID:
Dynamic

PIN:
*****   Reset

meeting options

☑ Allow unauthenticated callers to be the first people in a meeting. If not, then they will wait in the lobby until an authenticated user joins.

[save]   cancel

Figure 4-5. *Edit properties of the user for the audio conference*

The properties to set are as follows:

- *Provider name*: Choose your provider from the list.
  In this example, I've selected Microsoft.

Note   The remaining settings will apply only if you select Microsoft as the audio conferencing provider.

- *Default toll number*: For a third-party provider, these phone numbers are the ones you received from the audio conferencing provider. If the user is using Microsoft as the audio conferencing provider, these will be numbers that are set on the audio conferencing bridge. Format the numbers as you want them to appear in Skype for Business and Microsoft Teams meeting requests.

- *Default toll-free number*: For a third-party provider, these phone numbers are the ones you received from the audio conferencing provider. If the user is using Microsoft as the audio conferencing provider, these will be numbers that are set on the audio conferencing bridge. Format the numbers as you want them to appear in Skype for Business and Microsoft Teams meeting requests.

- *Send conference info via e-mail*: Click this link only if you want to immediately send an e-mail to the user with his or her conference ID and phone number. (This e-mail does not include the PIN.)

- *Conference ID*: Select Reset if you need to reset the conference ID for the user. Refer the Figure 4-5.

- *PIN*: Select Reset if you need to reset the PIN for the user.

- *Meeting Options*: Allow unauthenticated callers to be the first people in a meeting. Select this option to allow unauthenticated callers to be the first to join meetings.

Scheduling Audio Conference Meetings

Basically, audio conference scheduling is no different from scheduling a regular online meeting. When a user is assigned an Audio Conferencing license and the user creates a new Skype for Business or Microsoft Teams meeting in Outlook or Outlook on the Web (formerly OWA), the dial-in phone numbers and conferencing IDs are added to the meeting invite automatically.

After the audio conference is scheduled, there are two ways to start a meeting in which all the participants use a phone to dial-in:

- The meeting organizer needs to input his or her Audio Conferencing PIN to start the meeting. Callers get asked whether they wish to authenticate as the organizer of a given meeting when they dial the phone number of an online meeting. All participants who join the meeting via dial-in before the organizer starts will be placed in the lobby and will listen to music on hold. After the organizer starts the meeting by inputting his or her Audio Conferencing PIN, all participants in the lobby will automatically join the meeting.

- If the "Allow unauthenticated callers to be the first people in a meeting" setting (disabled by default) is enabled for a given organizer, then all meetings scheduled by that user will be able to be started without having the organizer input his or her Audio Conferencing PIN. When this setting is enabled, the meeting will start as soon as the first participant joins it via a dial-in phone number; that participant will not be put in the lobby.

A/V Call Setup and Media Flow

Microsoft Teams has different modalities like Audio/Video Call, Application sharing, meeting etc. For any modalities Teams client first connects to Office 365 Teams services for signaling where Teams client register and sign-in and connected. After users sign-in to Teams client can use features such as presence information, chat by using signaling protocol.

Then user can initiate calls using media. Every call involves signaling and media traffic. All Teams media traffic uses the Interactive Connectivity Establishment (ICE) protocol to find the most optimal media path between endpoints, just as Skype for Business does.

ICE is protocol that has all logic for connectivity. It uses two protocols: Session Traversal Utilities for NAT (STUN), which helps traverse the NAT device, and Traversal Using Relay NAT (TURN), which is used for relaying NAT. There are two types of relay: media relay and transport relay.

Media relay is built for on-premises Skype for Business Server (formerly known as Lync). Media relay runs on the edge server. And the same is used in Skype for Business Online cloud for online users.

Transport relay is designed for cloud services, such as Teams, and it has the scalability and flexibility to support cloud customers. Transport relays are much smarter than Media relay and use dynamic discovery in anycast IPs, which are based on location, so it will find and use a local relay server instead of a remote relay to keep traffic locally or regionally. Organizations must have Internet breakouts in order to use transport relay for Teams traffic.

Another difference is that media relay is static and used for one datacenter, whereas transport relay uses dynamic discovery via anycast IP addresses.

Using Interactive Connectivity Establishment

As I mentioned earlier, Teams media traffic uses the ICE protocol to find the most optimal media path between endpoints. Every endpoint uses ICE, including Teams desktop, mobile, Mac clients, and cloud service components. Modalities such as Audio, Video, and desktop sharing also use ICE.

The ICE process involves five phases:

1. *Sign-in Process*: . The Teams client requests credentials via a Transport Relay Authentication Provider (TRAP). Credential for Microsoft teams from Office 365 cloud services.

When establishing a call:

2. *Candidate Discovery*: In this phase, discovery occurs in order to find the candidate for media path on endpoint. Above figure shows, shows endpoints discover candidate from relay server for media.

Figure 4-6 shows candidate discovery process.

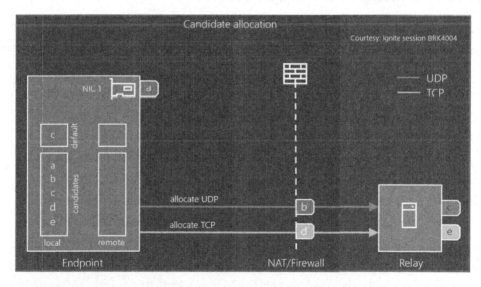

Figure 4-6. *Candidate discovery*

3. *Candidate Exchange*: In this phase, both the caller and the recipient endpoints will exchange the candidates.

4. *Connectivity Checks*: In this phase, the candidates exchanged between endpoints are used for connectivity checks. After the connectivity succeeds, the candidate connectivity checks stop.

5. *Candidate Promotion*: In this phase, the candidate gets promoted to establish the optimal media path for better quality.

What is the candidate? *Candidates* are a combination of IP addresses and ports potentially used for media connectivity. For example, if I want to call someone by using Teams, my Teams endpoint has to allocate a candidate from my computer—that is, my host IP address and port number—so the other party can potentially connect to it.

Understanding Connectivity

Say two endpoints are establishing connectivity with each other; the first endpoint is named A, and the second endpoint is B. First, both endpoints will connect to signaling (that is, the Office 365 cloud service), where endpoint can register and sign in to get signaling connectivity. After they sign in, they see each other as an online presence and can exchange instant messages if they want to talk to each other.

If they decide to establish an audio/video or desktop sharing call, the Teams client would like to send media as directly as possible. Obviously, Teams could send media to the Office 365 cloud and relay it from there. However, we don't want to do that because sending media to the Office 365 cloud may degrade the call quality because of the extra hop that media travels. So, we prefer to keep media as local as possible.

For example, if two users are sitting in same building but on different floors and they make a call, their audio media traffic will reach its endpoint faster by using a direct connection as compared to sending it over the Internet (Office 365 cloud), which may increase latency and result in dropped packets as well.

166

However, direct connectivity is always not possible; NAT devices or a firewall may not allow a direct connection, and that's a problem. If three people are sitting in different locations (for example, one is in a corporate office, the second is in a home office, and the third is in a hotel room), then their signaling always goes to the Office 365 cloud service. However, media will not go through directly, and most likely a firewall device will block media traffic, because this media could be any port from any random client, so why would a firewall allow connection to directly internal network.

Figure 4-7 shows, how NAT blocking traffic.

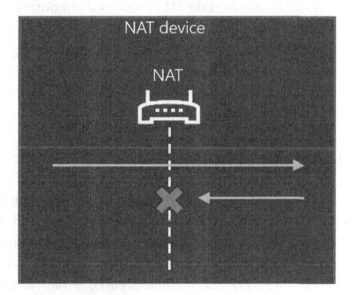

Figure 4-7. *NAT blocking traffic*

Understanding NAT

Network Address Translation (NAT) is used for one to many connections. For example, home Internet is a good example of NAT. Your home Internet provider is given a single public IP address, but all your laptop, phone, and iPad devices will have separate private IP addresses. This is possible through NAT, which is used by home routers (one IP address from the public Internet side, and many private IPs inside the router).

Private IP addresses get translated with a NAT public IP address. This is good, because we have multiple IP addresses, and traffic flows via one IP address with security, as random traffic will get allow by public IP address and random traffic gets drop by NAT device. However NAT drop Teams media traffic because NAT device will allow traffic that initiated by private IP addresses and drop incoming traffic.

A corporate firewall also blocks random traffic. This firewall has additional features such as deep packet inspection, which also blocks the direct traffic.

HTTP proxy servers also filter the HTTP requests. The proxy scans the downloads, which provides additional security. However, it affects Microsoft Teams and Skype for Business traffic because HTTP scanning might corrupt traffic and some customers block nonproxy traffic, including UDP.

The NAT, firewall, and proxy server may block traffic (direct). So the solution for this problem is ICE, STUN, and TURN, which I've mentioned.

Understanding Call Setup

The Teams client registers with Office 365 services, and signaling traffic traverse through Office 365 Teams services. Teams uses the REST API via HTTPS, and Teams uses WebSocket for more persistent communication. Teams media traffic prefers direct connectivity; however, direct connectivity is not always possible because of NAT, firewalls, and proxy devices. Direct connectivity is shown in Figure 4-8.

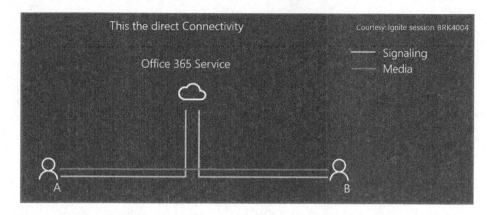

Figure 4-8. *Direct connectivity*

Whenever direct connectivity is not possible, the media is relayed through the Office 365 cloud service via transport relay. This process happens through ICE, similarly to the process used in Skype for Business. In Teams, STUN and TURN servers operate as relay servers. When one Teams client wants to talk to another Teams client but there is no direct connectivity, Teams always uses STUN and TURN servers to relay the audio media traffic. At the same time, these relay servers help to discover public IP addresses and allow NAT to accept incoming traffic.

The way it works is as follows: The Teams client sends a packet to the STUN and TURN servers. Then the relay server gets the message and allocates a candidate to the respective clients. Teams client connectivity sends the packet back to the client. The client gets the STUN address (public IP address). Then the internal client or host in the private network will get to know the public IP address of the NAT device, to accept the traffic there. Under the ICE process, candidates are exchanged between endpoints, and then endpoints determines the optimal media paths.

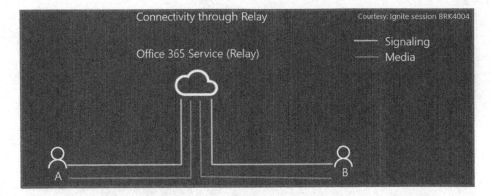

Figure 4-9. *The client uses the Office 365 service for signaling and media*

Figure 4-9 shows user A and user B, both connected to an Office 365 service for signaling and media. Media traffic is relayed using transport relay, because direct connectivity is not possible.

Teams Connectors and Customization

Connectors are the best way to add application content into Teams. Connectors enable you to alert your team of any new activity by posting messages to an existing Teams channel. Using the Teams connector in Flow, you can create workflows to automate complex processes while keeping your team in the loop about what's happening.

For example, you can track your team's progress in Trello or follow a Twitter hashtag. You can even build flows to monitor all activity on social media forums and alert your team about events that are unexpected or require action. You add actions to content by using actionable messages to complete a task in the channel.

With Teams apps, you can add your existing Office 365 connector or build a new one to include in Microsoft Teams.

There are many connectors available, as shown in Figure 4-10.

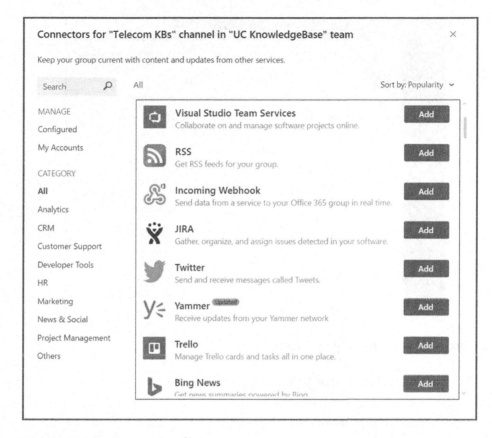

Figure 4-10. *Connector list*

Adding Connectors

Many built-in connectors are available for use, and administrators can create new custom connectors as well.

To add a connector, follow these steps:

1. Log on to Teams. Select the team for which you want to add a connector, and choose the More icon next to the channel name. Then select Connectors, as shown in Figure 4-11.

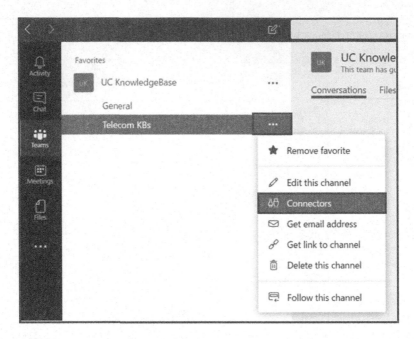

Figure 4-11. *Connector options*

2. You will see list of connectors under the All
    Connectors tab. Find the connector that will fulfill
    your requirements and then click Add, as shown in
    Figure 4-12.

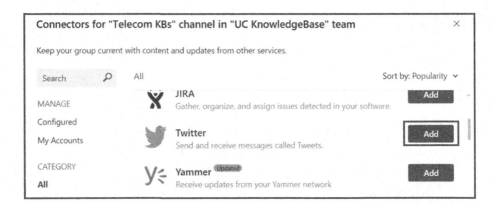

Figure 4-12. *Adding a connector*

You have to configure the connector that you are adding; follow the process onscreen. In this example, you're adding a Twitter connector.

Creating Custom Webhooks

If you want to create an incoming webhook connector, follow these steps;

1. Log on to Microsoft Teams. Expand the team and select More options (…) next to the channel name. Then click Connectors.

2. Find the Incoming Webhook option from the list of connectors and click Add, as shown in Figure 4-13.

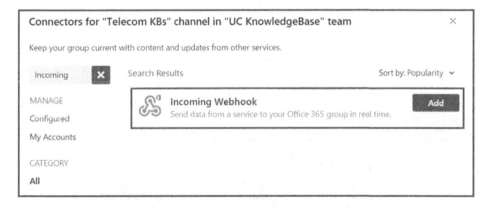

Figure 4-13. *Adding the incoming webhook*

3. After you click Add, a new window will open; click Install.

4. Another new page opens that allows you to input information. Give a meaningful name to the webhook and add a relevant image to identify the webhook correctly. Then click Create, as shown in Figure 4-14.

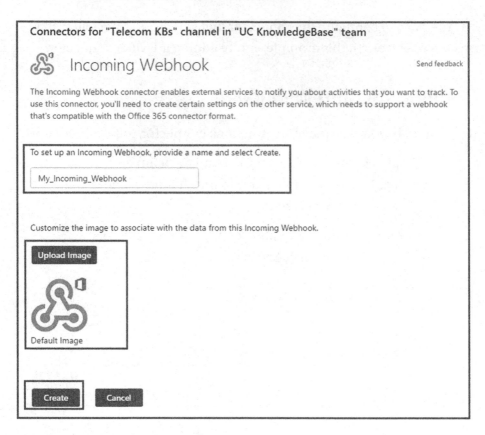

Figure 4-14. *Creating a webhook*

5. Copy the webhook information, because we'll need the webhook URL for sending information to Teams.

    Figure 4-15 shows Webhook URL.

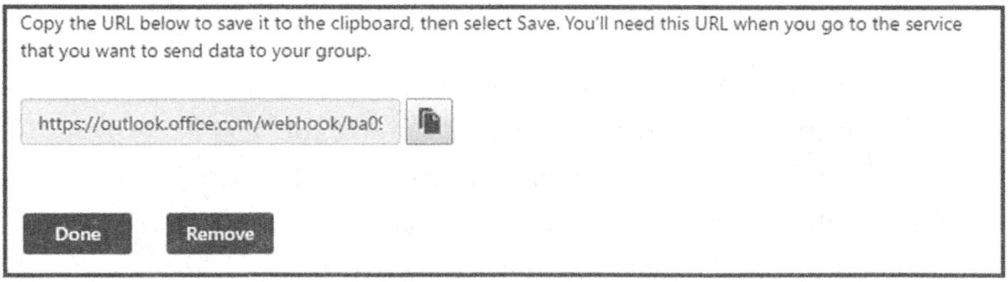

Copy the URL below to save it to the clipboard, then select Save. You'll need this URL when you go to the service that you want to send data to your group.

    https://outlook.office.com/webhook/ba0⏿

    Done   Remove

Figure 4-15. *Webhook URL*

6.   Click the Done button to complete this process.

On Teams, you can see a message indicating that the incoming webhook was created, as shown in Figure 4-16.

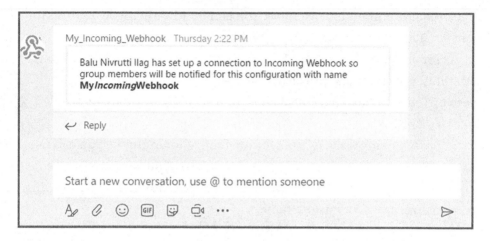

Figure 4-16. *The webhook shows in the channel*

Registering a Connector

Once you have a connector created, make sure to register it so that you can distribute the connector as part of your app package. These connectors can be used in Teams; you can package and publish them as part of your AppSource submission, or you can provide them to users directly for uploading within Teams.

To distribute the connector, you need to register it by using the Connectors Developer Dashboard. To have your connector work in Microsoft Teams, select Microsoft Teams under Enable This Integration For.

After enabling integration, click Save in the Connectors Developer Dashboard, and your Connector is registered.

To learn more about connectors, refer to `https://docs.microsoft.com/en-us/microsoftteams/platform/concepts/connectors`.

Built-in and Custom Tabs

Tabs can bring web-based content straight into your team channels. Tabs are like web pages that are integrated in Teams. You can register them in Teams by using a manifest file. In other words, you can think of tabs as web pages that are embedded in Teams. You can build a Microsoft Teams tab from scratch or adapt your existing web-app experience.

As I mentioned in Chapter 3, tabs are great way to extend your Teams capabilities in channels. However, these are not simply standard tabs; these are custom tabs that you can use to show dynamic data on web pages.

There are many use cases of tabs for Teams; for example, you can use tabs for dashboards to showcase data, for details about support incidents, , and for YouTube videos that provide some sort of training. The following are some use cases for custom tabs:

- Dashboards

- Details pages

- Training videos

- Consoles

Now, another thing that you can do with tabs is to provide deep links to items. For example, you could have a description of a task and add a link about that description as a tab.

Adding Tabs to a Channel

Adding tabs to channels is easy:

1. Log on to Microsoft Teams. Click the Teams option and then expand the teams to see the channel names.

2. Choose the channel name that you want to open.
    Then click the plus sign, which will allow you to add
    tabs, as shown in Figure 4-17.

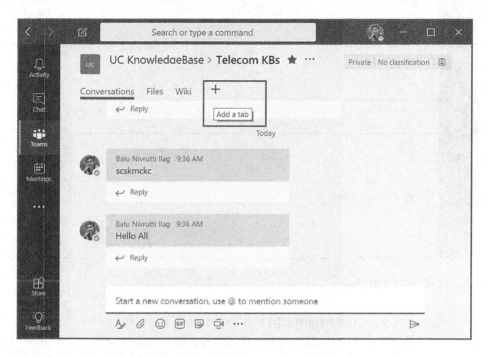

Figure 4-17. *Addding a tab*

3. After clicking Add a Tab, you will see a list of tabs
    available by default. Choose the tab that you want to
    add; in Figure 4-18, I've chosen the Planner tab.

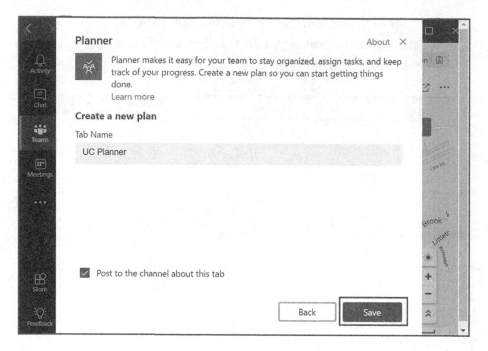

Figure 4-18. *Tab list*

4. Give your tab a name. In this example, I've set the name to UC planner. Then click Save Now. You'll see UC Planner added as a tab in your channel.

Tabs have two scopes:

- *Team scope*: These tabs are for teams. Team-scope tabs in a channel allow teams to interact and have shared experiences. All tabs in channels are configurable, so users can configure the content of a tab experience when the tab is first added to a channel.

- *Personal scope*: These tabs are for individual users. Personal-scope tabs allow users to interact with the experience privately. The tab content is static and relevant to individual users.

In addition, you can divide tabs into two types:

- *Configurable tabs (team scope)*: This type of tab will be part of a channel and provide a single kind of information to a team. For example, the Planner tab for a channel contains a single plan for the entire team. This tab requires a configuration page.

  To learn more about configuration pages, refer to

  `https://docs.microsoft.com/en-us/ microsoftteams/platform/concepts/tabs/tabs- configuration.`

- *Static tab (personal scope)*: A static tab is a content page that is declared directly in a manifest and does not require a configuration page.

  Currently, you can add one or more static tabs to your apps as a personal-scope experience, accessed via the app bar or alongside your app's bot conversation.

  To learn more about static pages, refer to `https:// docs.microsoft.com/en-us/microsoftteams/ platform/concepts/tabs/tabs-static.`

Updating or Removing a Microsoft Teams Tab

You can modify a tab after it has been added. You also can rename or remove a tab from the team channel.

Open Teams, choose the channel name, and then right-click the tab's name to rename or remove it, as shown in Figure 4-19.

Note   Conversations and Files are default tabs that cannot be removed.

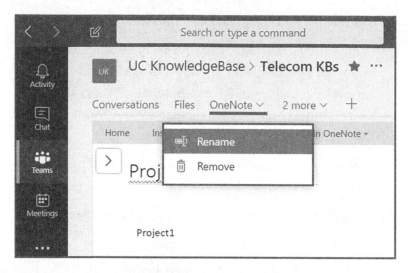

Figure 4-19. *Removing or updating tabs*

In this example, we're removing a OneNote tab. After selecting to remove the tab, you'll be asked for confirmation. Click the Remove button to permanently delete the OneNote tab, as shown in Figure 4-20.

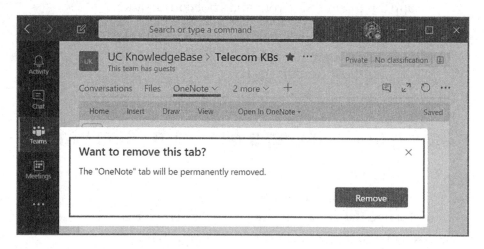

Figure 4-20. *Removing tabs*

Note   Supporting removal options can significantly improve the user experience, especially if you expect users to frequently add and remove your tabs. However, there is no guarantee that your page will always be loaded when a tab is removed. For example, the page won't be loaded if the user deletes the entire team or channel in which your tab sits.

Microsoft Teams for Education Sector

Microsoft Teams is a digital hub that brings conversations, content, and apps together in one place. Educators can create collaborative classrooms, connect in professional learning communities, and communicate with school staff, all from a single experience in Office 365 for Education.

Helping students engage with technology, making resources available at their fingertips, communication, collaboration, critical thinking, and creativity—Teams does all of that. It's really a new way for schools to connect and collaborate. Teams is highly collaborative because conversations can be in real-time as well as more informal and more consistent. We have the ability to bring in apps such as OneNote, and to have face-to-face conversations by adding video.

Teams is a conversation-based work place. With Teams, school staff and students can collaborate in one location. After they log in to Teams by using the Office 365 portal on an education tenant, users can see apps, files, chats, meetings, calls and added contacts. They can easily create their own teams as well.

The following types of preconfigured Teams templates are available, and educators can select from them while creating teams:

- *Classes*: Teachers and students collaborating on group projects, assignments, and more

- *PLCs*: Educators collaborating within a professional learning community, or PLC

- *Staff Members*: Staff leaders and staff members collaborating on school administration and development

- *Anyone*: Students and school users collaborating in interest groups and clubs

In Teams, users can create files, have conversations, and upload existing files and other learning materials. Frequently used apps can be added as tabs in Teams for easy access. For example, educators who are using OneNote frequently can simply add OneNote as a tab right there in the team channel,

Channels are topics that have separate aspects of each task or work. Example, Units of Data, student study projects or school cultural information can be sees as channels. Team members can jump into a conversation at any time. They can have threaded chats for easy-to-track conversations relevant to educators. Team member can embed files, stickers, images, emoticons, and even third-party connectors or bots for a truly integrated experience.

Teams also help teachers and students stay on schedule by using meeting tabs. Meeting features bring Outlook calendars into one digital hub. Teachers and students can have online meetings that are scheduled or ad hoc.

Accessing Teams apps doesn't require platform dependency. Educators and learners have the opportunity to engage with Teams from any device, including iOS, Android, Windows, and Mac, using the

Microsoft Teams client app or web apps anytime. Conversations can move around when students are at the playground, on a field trip, or waiting for the school bus, by using Teams from a mobile device.

School staff can accomplish work more efficiently, because collaborating via Teams doesn't require a specific time or place. Users can have a conversation or discussion anytime, anyplace, using their mobile devices. Teams brings everything into one digital hub.

Creating a Class in Microsoft Teams

Microsoft listened to school leaders, teachers, IT professionals, and even students from around the world to create a whole new classroom experience built into Office 365. The classroom experience in Microsoft Teams builds on existing Office 365 apps. It saves educators time by making learning more personalized, integrated, and accessible inside and outside the classroom.

Before logging in to teams, you must enable your education Office 365 tenant for Microsoft Teams.

Remember, as I mentioned, Microsoft Teams is available for all education customers as part of the Office 365 for Education suite licensing: Education, Education Plus, and Education E5, as well as existing Education E3 suites.

Here is the admin guide for enabling teams for your Office 365 tenant: `https://support.office.com/en-us/article/microsoft-teams-getting-started-guide-for-it-admins-e7b992dc-de27-4303-8973-7a1ca8ad7cfb`.

To create a class in Teams, follow these steps:

1. Log on to a Teams apps or web page (`https://teams.microsoft.com`).

2. Click the Teams option and then click Create or Join Teams.

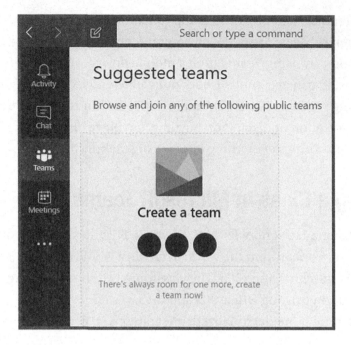

Figure 4-21. *Creating a team*

3. Click Create a Team, as shown in Figure 4-21. You will see various options for creating teams. These are templates to create the respective teams. Figure 4-22 shows the template options.

Figure 4-22. *Selecting a Teams template*

4.   Choose the team type Classes. This template will
     help teachers and students collaborate on group
     projects, assignments, and more.

Now it's time to give a meaningful name to the team and complete the
team creation process.

Classes automatically come with tabs for OneNotebook that can be
used as a class notebook. Teachers can access data, share files, create
assignments, and distribute material with personalize groups. Anytime
group can prefer chat verses talk, they can use the Meet Now option to
jump on a call with audio/video capabilities and application-sharing
capabilities. There is no need to switch applications, because all of this is
happening in the same window.

The classroom experiences in Microsoft Teams build on existing
Office 365 apps. This saves educators time by making learning more
personalized, integrated, and accessible inside and outside the classroom.

After teams have been created and are available, a student can be
enrolled as a member. Classes can be automatically populated by student
rosters from the school's information system. In addition, users can easily
move files into Microsoft Teams.

Creating a channel for a specific purpose or task and naming it based
on a certain subject, topic, or discipline is up to the teacher. The following
are some example topics:

- Earth science

- Math assignment

- Language test

- Physical science

A teacher can update class data from their computer to the Teams site
or move all kinds of files, including Word documents, OneNote data, and
PowerPoint presentations from an existing OneDrive or SharePoint site to
Teams.

They can also place files or tabs under a specific channel. Clicking the channel enables access to all available tabs: Conversations for class discussions, Files, and Class Notes are already present, so there's no need to add them.

If users want to add a new tab, they simply click the plus sign and select the required tabs.

Using Teams for Teachers

Microsoft Teams provides ideas and suggestions to help educators manage their daily workflow (classroom practices). Because educators are constantly looking for ways to minimize the amount of time spent on administrative tasks that take valuable time away from working with students, Microsoft Teams helps in doing this.

While working with students, teachers can start a conversation tab enabling students to ask questions or discuss the topic being taught; students can even ask and resolve each other's questions. This is also a great way to keep a group of students on task when the teacher is working with an individual student.

When using Teams, sharing files and student material is also easy. Before sharing materials, make sure that you are on the right class and channel, and then select files and simply upload them to the class files.

Class Notebook is another great way to manage content delivery and provide a place for collaboration and keep up with student work, all within a notebook.

Each unit can have a tab in the content section. Student can do problem-based learning, student divided in to problem-based learning group and collaboration space. The teacher can monitor every student's work and tests in the student section. Each student has a private notebook that the teacher can access and use to provide individual feedback.

Managing assignments is a snap, and using teams is keep the front of every student whenever they are on Office 365. Teams makes students less likely to lose assignments or to forget to do them. Everything needed for assignments is available there on Teams.

As students turn in their work, the teacher can easily see who has completed the work and who has not. The teacher can add feedback and grade the student.

The teacher also can easily monitor the progress of each student individually. The teacher can see an assignment as soon as it's submitted by the student. Another feature for teachers pertains to workflow; for example, posting something or replying to a thread someone started. This makes class workflow more efficient, by allowing the teacher and student to ask questions to a specific person or make a comment virtually. When a student likes a comment posted by a teacher, that teacher knows that the comments have been read by the student. A numbers or notification appears in the activity icon. As at symbol appears on Teams icon.

Teams provides many advantages, such as the following:

- All students are in one location. So, there's no need to find student details in different places.

- Classwork is organized in channels and tabs to facilitate student learning.

- It's easy to make, monitor, evaluate, and return assignments to students.

- Conversations between teachers and students, or students and students, can help clarify assignments or work collaboratively.

Using Microsoft Teams, students' and teachers' daily tasks have become a lot easier.

Using Professional Learning Communities

PLCs are most effective when there is an organized way to meet, learn, and grow professionally. Microsoft Teams provides that medium, to bring educators together in person or virtually, so they can discuss, share, learn, and grow professionally, all the while keeping resources and communications at the educator's fingertips.

PLCs can help educators meet student achievement targets as well as keep everyone organized and learning collaboratively.

Use the following steps to create a professional learning community team:

1. Log in to the Office 365 portal. Click the Teams app. Open the Teams app in a browser or on the Teams client installed on your computer.

2. Click the Teams option and then click Create or Join Teams. Click the Create Teams option and then choose PLCs, as shown in Figure 4-23.

Figure 4-23. PLC teams

3. Give your team a name, such as Fourth Grade
    Professional Learning Communities. In this
    example, shown in Figure 4-24, all fourth-grade
    teachers will be working together to set this PLC to
    private, because they are going to share students'
    test scores with each other.

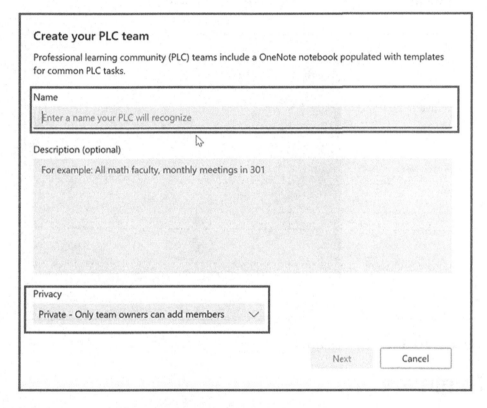

Figure 4-24. *Naming your PLC teams*

Whether teachers are meeting in person or virtually, it is important to get their meeting set up. There are two easy ways to meet people easily and effectively: when teachers click on a meeting, they have the opportunity to set a meeting, and the meeting invite looks like an Outlook invite. In fact, a meeting invite appears in your Outlook calendar just like Skype meeting.

If teacher want to discuss topics with your PLC teams, you can immediately create a Meet Now for whoever is online and jump into a conversation or share documents. Also, teachers can see team members' availability by using small, green circle with a checkmark at the bottom corner of their picture.

To create a PLC file, they can use a OneNote notebook, which has preconfigured PLC template in it, as shown in Figure 4-25.

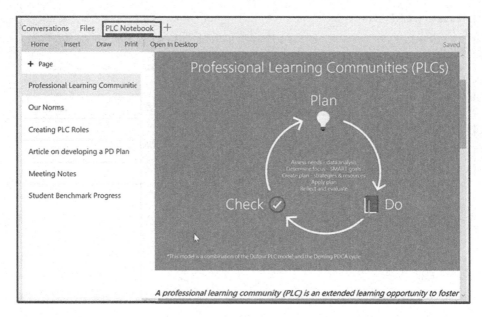

Figure 4-25. *PLCs notebook*

Summary

This chapter covers Teams capabilities, such as audio conferencing. Office 365 allows conference participants to join Teams meetings from any telephone, including mobile and landline phones, without Internet access. In Teams, every call involves signaling and media traffic. All Teams media traffic uses the Interactive Connectivity Establishment (ICE) protocol to find the most optimal media path between endpoints. Connectors are the best way to add application content into Teams, and you can add existing Office 365 connectors to Teams. Tabs bring web-based content straight into team channels. Tabs are like web pages that are integrated in Teams; you can register them into Teams by using a manifest file. Using Teams, educators can create collaborative classrooms, connect in professional learning communities, and communicate with school staff, all from a single experience in Office 365 for Education.

CHAPTER 5

Journey from Skype for Business to Microsoft Teams

This chapter provides detailed steps that will help you prepare your organization for Microsoft Teams and complete the journey from Skype for Business to Teams. This chapter covers the following topics:

1. The journey from Skype for Business to Microsoft Teams

2. Optimizing an existing Skype for Business server environment for Teams

3. Migration path from Skype for Business to Microsoft Teams

4. Using Microsoft Teams and Skype for Business side by side

5. Piloting Teams alongside Skype for Business

6. Driving Microsoft Teams user adoption

7. Microsoft Teams roadmap

© Balu N Ilag 2018
B.N. Ilag, *Introducing Microsoft Teams*, https://doi.org/10.1007/978-1-4842-3567-6_5

Journey from Skype for Business to Microsoft Teams

As you know, Microsoft announced last year that Skype for Business capabilities would be built into Microsoft Teams. This will happen over time; ultimately, Microsoft Teams will become the single client experience.

This does not mean that there will be no Skype for Business investment. Skype for Business Server 2015 will have a successor called Skype for Business Server 2019 (which is planned for the second half of 2018). Skype for Business will remain the client for Skype for Business Server. As you know, Microsoft Teams has a lot of collaboration features that Skype for Business does not have. And from a communication perspective, Teams is catching up to Skype for Business.

However, there is no real migration from one product to another. The two products are built separately and this moreover transaction from one to another product. Microsoft has been adding new capabilities to Teams, and eventually Teams will become the only UC client. When Teams has all the features that Skype for Business has, Teams will become the successor of Skype for Business (see Figure 5-1). That's why I said there is no real migration. But this is a long journey, and organizations have to be ready for Teams in order to have success. This chapter will help you become ready for Teams.

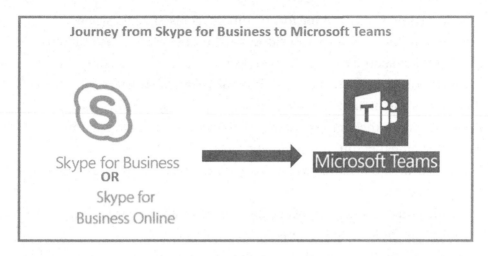

Figure 5-1. *The journey from Skype for Business to Microsoft Teams*

Microsoft has already added instant messaging (chat), persistent chat, audio/video calls, audio conferencing, online meetings, and many more features to Teams. Microsoft is continuing to enhance the team experience and to build Skype for Business capabilities into Teams.

Microsoft Teams is being built on a new, modern Skype infrastructure for enterprise-grade voice and video communications. Microsoft's next-generation cloud-born architecture is already powering communication experiences in Teams and is evolving rapidly.

Before a meeting, Teams can present relevant documents and rich information about the participants to help you prepare. During a meeting, the conversation can be captured, transcribed, and time-coded, with closed captioning and voice recognition for attributing remarks to specific individuals.

After a meeting, the cloud recording and transcript can be automatically added to the relevant channel, so conversations, documents, notes, and action items can be reviewed, indexed, and searched by the entire team.

There is no fixed deadline for customers needs to move Skype for Business Online or Skype for Business On-Premises to Microsoft Teams. Microsoft has shared the roadmap for Microsoft Teams availability, so that organizations can assess the capabilities of Microsoft Teams relative to their needs and plan their move to Teams. The roadmap shows Microsoft's expectations for the timing of new Teams features, so organizations can determine their timing for moving to Microsoft Teams in a way that best meets their needs. You can find the roadmap at `https://aka.ms/ skype2teamsroadmap`.

In this transformation process, the key is to start preparing your organization for Microsoft Teams. Many things are going to remain as is, such as your current network connectivity (wired and wireless), firewall/ proxy device, end-user workstations, mobile devices, and organizational policies. For a healthy Teams implementation, you must be sure to validate these things before even thinking about a Teams implementation.

This chapter will help you drive this environment readiness and help validate your current Skype for Business or any other UC environment to prepare for Teams deployment.

Optimizing the Existing Skype for Business Environment for Microsoft Teams

Teams is not completely ready to provide an enterprise UC experience like Skype for Business. However, preparing your environment for Teams is necessary so that your organization can be fully ready for Teams when the time comes.

As part of moving from Skype for Business to Microsoft Teams, you must continue investing in network readiness; Teams will directly benefit from all improvements that you make in network quality for Skype for Business. You can begin exploring Teams today to understand the value it can offer to your organization, while you continue to run Skype for Business.

Start with Network Validation

Environment preparation should start with your network, because the network is the backbone of any real-time communication product. Performing a network readiness assessment is necessary even if you are already running a real-time communication product such as Skype for Business, Jabber, or Google Hangouts.

Microsoft has its own tool for a network readiness test. This tool covers network performance, network planning, and other general networking aspects such as ports and protocols that must be allowed. Also, you can get help from Microsoft for this, by referring to its Network Readiness Assessment guide (`https://go.microsoft.com/fwlink/?linkid=859069`).

Here are the main aspects of a network readiness assessment:

You must have some product knowledge and require a toolset for planning and managing Teams and Skype for Business to have operation success. Microsoft offers guidance through My Advisor (`http://aka.ms/myadvisor`).

Before starting a pilot for Teams, check your existing call quality with a real-time communication product and make a baseline. If you have Skype for Business deployed, you can use the Call Quality Dashboard (both for on-premises and Skype for Business Online) to monitor usage and identify quality trends, and Call Analytics in order to look at quality indicators of individual calls.

After completing the network readiness assessment, you can engage with Microsoft to conduct an Office 365 network performance assessment. This focuses on the network infrastructure used to connect to Office 365 services, to ensure it is connecting and performing as efficiently as possible.

The Microsoft Network Assessment Tool provides the ability to perform a simple test of network performance to determine how well the network would perform for a Microsoft Teams or Skype for Business call. The tool tests the connection to the Microsoft network edge by streaming a set of packets to the nearest edge site and back for approximately 17 seconds for a configured number of iterations. This tool reports the following:

- Packet loss

- Jitter

- Round-trip latency

- Reorder packet percentage

- Sent and received packets

Basically, this tool provides the ability to verify network connectivity between the test location and the Microsoft network. The tool also checks whether port numbers and IP addresses are correctly configured to enable communication for a Microsoft Teams call. Test results provide comprehensive information on which scenarios passed and which didn't. When the Network Assessment Tool starts, it initializes an audio call and waits 17 seconds before ending the call. The tool will capture the packet loss, round-trip time, packets sent, packets received, and average jitter. Also, this test shows reachability to the relay server over UDP and TCP, and finally it will show which tests passed and which didn't.

Analyzing the call quality is equally important, because it doesn't matter how well your network is configured if end users are facing call-quality issues. , A Call Quality Dashboard (CQD) is available to monitor usage and identify quality trends, and Call Analytics can help you troubleshoot or look at quality indicators of individual calls.

You can refer to the Microsoft CQD training video to understand the Call Quality Dashboard as well as tips and tricks (`www.skypeoperations framework.com/Academy?SOFTrainings=Leverage%20the%20Investigate% 20Media%20Quality%20using%20CQD%20Videos`) and check Call Analytics by using audio/video (`https://support.office.com/article/Set-up-Skype-for-Business-Call-Analytics-fbf7247a-84ae-46cc-9204-2c45b1c734cd`).

Teams has different dependencies other than the network. You should make sure that all dependent services also work as expected, As I mentioned earlier, Teams is a hub of communication and collaboration that combines multiple Office 365 cloud services. Therefore, Teams is dependent on other services, such as SharePoint Online, Exchange Online, and OneDrive for Business. For a successful Teams implementation, these dependent services must provide an optimal experience for users. So, you must validate these dependent services or applications.

Implement Quality of Service for Microsoft Teams

What is *Quality of Service* (QoS), and why do we need it in Teams? Quality of Service is a process of prioritizing specific types of network traffic by using port ranges, protocols, and applications. There are different ways to implement QoS. When planning for Microsoft Teams, you must look to prioritize Teams-specific traffic in order to optimize the user experience. I must admit that QoS is not the only solution to every call-quality problem, but QoS uses a combination of networking technologies to enable organizations to optimize the end-user experience for real-time audio, video, and application-sharing communications.

QoS is commonly used when network bandwidth is limited and when network congestion, in practice bandwidth limitation and network congestion always there so we must have QoS configure correctly to optimize the end-user experience.

QoS is more effective when it's configured end to end—meaning from the user computer where the Microsoft Teams client is running, to network switches, to the router, to the Office 365 cloud—complete end-to-end signaling and a media path. If any path doesn't support QoS, that could degrade the entire Teams call quality.

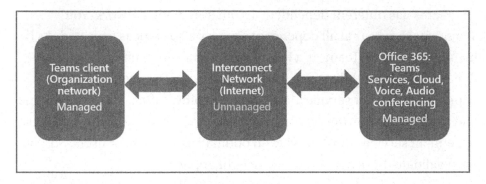

Figure 5-2. *Quality of Service*

As shown in Figure 5-2, the organization's network is an on-premises network (which is a completely managed network) that is connected to an interconnect network (which is an unmanaged network) that is connected to the Office 365 cloud (Teams services—which is again a Microsoft-managed network).

For QoS implementation include two parts first customer implemented QoS on their managed (internal) network and second Microsoft has QoS implemented on their Office 365 Cloud network. But to have an end-to-end QoS interconnected network must honor QoS however it is not honor QoS, to solve this, there is ExpressRoute from Microsoft which can be an option for interconnected network to honor QoS to have end-to-end call quality.

I recommend implementing QoS on your organization-managed network where your users reside, even though you are not using ExpressRoute for the interconnect network and there is no control on it.

Implementing QoS on the organization's network will increase call quality for one-to-one calls between users. As shown in Figure 5-3, media traffic itself prefers to go directly and singling via Teams services. So, implementing QoS on your management network will increase call quality for all calls within your network.

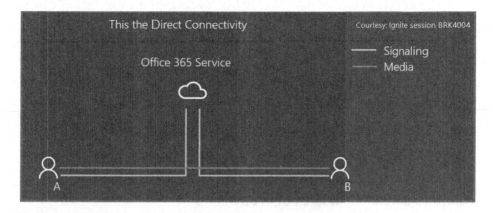

Figure 5-3. *Direct call connectivity*

There are multiple ways to prioritize traffic. However, the most common way is by using Differentiated Service Code Point (DSCP) marking. DSCP values can be applied based on port ranges and via a Group Policy Object. For Microsoft Teams, you must use both, because Group Policy Object (QoS-based) policies work only for Windows-domain-joined machines. A Teams client installed on a Windows machine will mark the traffic with DSCP values, but macOS, iOS, and Android devices will not mark Teams traffic with DSCP values. to do so implementing QoS via port-based tagging using network devices will work for non-Windows devices, which mark DSCP values by network devices using port ranges means configuring correct port ranges will be key for Quality of Service.

QoS Implementation Scenarios

This section details four QoS implementation scenarios:

- *Scenario 1*: Microsoft Teams is deployed or in the deploying stage, and you are planning on implementing QoS via port-based tagging. Port-based tagging is the most reliable method because it works universally throughout all platforms and is the easiest to implement.

- *Scenario 2*: Microsoft Teams is deployed or is in the deploying stage, and you are planning to implement QoS via Group Policy Object tagging.

Note   That QoS via Group Policy Object will work only for domain-joined Windows clients. Any device that is not a Windows domain-joined client will not be enabled for QoS\DSCP tagging. That's why Scenario 1 and 2 combined works better for Windows and non-Windows devices for QoS/DSCP marking.

- *Scenario 3*: Skype for Business Online is deployed, including QoS tagging, and you are now deploying Teams. Then you don't have to make any changes, because Teams will respect the existing configuration and will use the same port ranges and tagging traffic as the Skype for Business client.

- *Scenario 4*: Skype for Business on-premises is deployed, including QoS tagging, and you're now deploying Teams. You need to modify your existing QoS policies to add Teams.exe with new port ranges for audio, video, application sharing, and file transfer. Table 5-1 lists port ranges and DSCP values.

Table 5-1. *Recommended Port Ranges with DSCP Values and Class*

Client Traffic Type	Port Range Start	Port Range End	DSCP Value	DSCP Class
Audio	50000	50019	46	Expedited Forwarding (EF)
Video	50020	50039	34	Assured Forwarding (AF41)
Application sharing	50040	50059	18	Class Selector (CS3)
File transfer	50040	50059	18	Class Selector (CS3)

I strongly recommend using scenarios 1 and 2 together to accommodate Windows computer/devices and non-Windows devices including macOS, iOS, Android, and so forth.

Configure QoS for Teams

Follow these steps to configure QoS for Teams:

1. Configure port ranges to mark traffic on network devices. Your network devices such as a router will mark Teams unmarked traffic that is coming from macOS, iOS, and Android devices using correct port ranges—for example, audio traffic (50000–50019 with DSCP 46), video traffic (50020–50039 with DSCP 34), and app-sharing and file-transfer ports (50040–50059 with DSCP 18). So, Teams media traffic will get prioritized.

2. Configure policy-based QoS in Group Policy Object policies for Teams:

    a. Log in to the domain controller or computer that has Group Policy Management installed and open gpmc.msc.

    b. Open the Group Policy Management Editor. Expand the Computer Configuration option; expand Policies; and expand Windows Settings. Right-click policy-based QoS and then click Create New Policy, as shown in Figure 5-4.

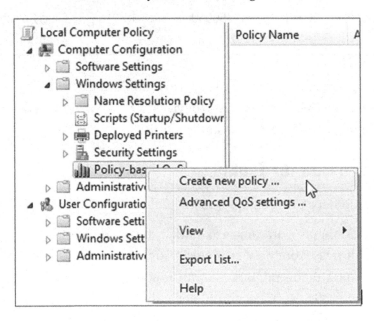

Figure 5-4. *Policy-based QoS*

    c. On Policy-Based QoS page, type policy name like, Teams-Audio and then set the DSCP Value as 46. On Next screen configure the application name as teams.exe and the port and protocol to UDP and TCP, with port range 50000-50019 for Teams audio.

    d.   Repeat steps b and c for video, application sharing, and file transfer, with respective port ranges and DSCP values.

3.   Finally, for testing, make Teams audio/video calls and capture network traffic by using Wireshark (`www.wireshark.org/download.html`) or NetMon (`https://www.microsoft.com/en-us/download/details.aspx?id=4865`). Analyze traffic or open the Registry and find the QoS policy keys.

    a.   Using the Registry on a Windows machine, open `regedit`. Browse to the path and validate QoS settings for `HKEY_LOCAL_MACHINE\SOFTWARE\Policies\Microsoft\Windows\QoS`.

    b.   Using Wireshark, make an audio call with another internal Teams user. Capture network traffic to check whether QoS tagging shows correctly. Verify two-way packets and see whether the DSCP value shows correctly.

Migration Path from Skype for Business to Microsoft Teams

As I mentioned earlier, there is no straightforward way to migrate users from Skype for Business to Microsoft Teams.

Before planning for migration, you must check your organization's business needs and see whether all required feature sets are available in Microsoft Teams, and then prepare your environment for Microsoft Teams.

A couple of options are available as part of migration. Complete details are presented next.

Path 1: Skype for Business On-Premises to Microsoft Teams

Two options are available as part of a migration from Skype for Business on-premises to Microsoft Teams. These options are not mandatory, and you're not limited to using only these options. In the future, Microsoft may introduce different migration options or strategies to simplify the migration work. The two options are as follows:

- Skype for Business on-premises to Microsoft Teams

- Skype for Business Online to Microsoft Teams

Microsoft Teams is a cloud-only solution. Before planning user migration from Skype for Business to Microsoft Teams, check whether the Microsoft Teams available features fulfill your business needs. To check the available features, refer to Table 5-2. If Teams has all the required features to fulfill your business needs, then start planning your Skype for Business on-premises migration to Microsoft Teams.

First you have to configure Teams from a purely on-premises environment to a hybrid environment, where a user's identity is available on both the cloud and on-premises. The Organization have Skype for Business On-premise environment they must configure their Skype for Business environment for Hybrid.

This is book doesn't cover how to configure the Skype for Business environment or the hybrid environment. If you are interested in configuring a hybrid environment, refer to the blog article at https:// blogs.technet.microsoft.com/canitpro/2015/12/23/step-by-step-skype-for-business-2015-hybrid-configuration/.

Once you have the Skype for Business Hybrid environment up and running, that means all your Skype for Business on-premises users sync with Azure Active Directory and available under Office 365 tenant in active users, assign the appropriate license to users to use Skype for Business Online. Microsoft Teams Licensing is covered in Chapter 1.

Before starting business user migration, run the pilot user migration. For the pilot, gather users from IT support teams, projects teams, and actual business users who are actively participating in pilot testing and are ready to provide their experience. Then start migrating the pilot Skype for Business on-premises user to Skype for Business Online. Later, gather users' feedback.

As I mentioned earlier, there is no direct migration path from Skype for Business on-premises to Microsoft Teams that can take your existing Skype for Business users' data to Microsoft Teams in the cloud. Instead, customers may use this migration path: Skype for Business on-premises to Skype for Business Online to Microsoft Teams, as shown in Figure 5-5. Microsoft may introduce new and simplified migration options in the future.

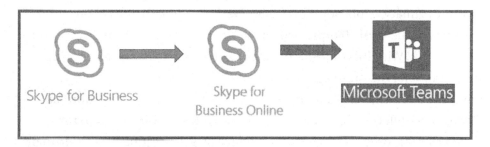

Figure 5-5. *Migration paths from Skype for Business on-premises to Microsoft Teams*

First, migrate users from Skype for Business on-premises to Skype for Business Online. Test and validate all functionality and then, finally, move users from Skype for Business Online to Microsoft Teams.

Note   It is not mandatory to migrate users from Skype for Business to Skype for Business Online. Customers can start using Microsoft Teams side by side with Skype for Business on-premises as well.

Use Direct Routing to Move Your Skype for Business On-Premises Phone System to Microsoft Teams

Again, this is not the only option available, and it is not mandatory to migrate users from Skype for Business on-premises to Skype for Business Online. Customers can start using Microsoft Teams side by side with Skype for Business, and then slowly move all their workload to Microsoft Teams from Skype for Business. Then support teams can introduce Microsoft Teams as a phone system using direct routing.

In this option, the organization must introduce Microsoft Teams to users so that users can start using Microsoft Teams for chat, audio/video calls and meetings, and file content—side by side with Skype for Business. After users are familiar with Microsoft Teams and are ready to use Teams as their primary application for their needs, then the organization can start using Microsoft Teams as its primary phone system with direct route capabilities. With this option, the organization can leverage its existing investment for on-premises PSTN, including SIP trunk, session border controller, and Internet telephony service provider long-term contracts. There is no different licenses requirement for Microsoft Teams to use direct routing, organization who has Office 365 E3 + Cloud PBX add-on or Office 365 E5 license which work for direct routing.

Direct Routing in Microsoft Teams

Direct routing is a feature for routing phone calls to Microsoft Teams in the Office 365 cloud (see Figure 5-6). For direct routing customers, the existing Internet telephony service provider, SIP trunk, or PRI line will be terminated at the customer's infrastructure session border controller (SBC), where all phone number ranges are configured, including transformation rules and route logic Then, through the Internet, the customer SBC will connect to Microsoft Teams and the phone system in

208

the Office 365 cloud. Customers can leverage ExpressRoute to connect the SBC to the Microsoft Teams phone system in the Office 365 cloud.

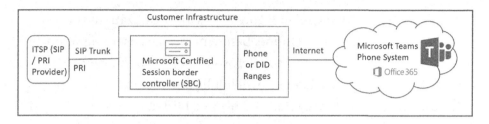

Figure 5-6. *Using direct route for Microsoft Teams phone system*

As of March 2018, direct routing works only with Microsoft Teams. Organizations using Skype for Business Online can continue using Cloud Connector Edition (CCE).

Call Flows Using Direct Routing

Caller ➤ Inbound Phone call: Internet Telephony Service Provider (Carrier) ➤ Session Border Controller (Customer SBC) ➤ Microsoft Teams Phone System (Office 365) ➤ Teams users as Receiver.

Outbound Phone call flow: Microsoft Teams user ➤ Microsoft Teams Phone System (Office 365) ➤ Session Border Controller (Customer SBC) ➤ Internet Telephony Service Provider (Carrier) ➤ Receiver.

Refer Microsoft announcement for direct routing: https://techcommunity.microsoft.com/t5/Microsoft-Teams-Blog/Direct-Routing-enables-new-enterprise-voice-options-in-Microsoft/ba-p/170450

Path 2: Skype for Business Online to Microsoft Teams

This migration path, depicted in Figure 5-7, is for organizations that are using Skype for Business Online. Before planning a user migration from Skype for Business Online to Microsoft Teams, check whether the Microsoft Teams available features will fulfill your business needs. To check the available features, refer to Table 5-2. I If Teams has all required features to fulfill your business needs, start planning your Skype for Business Online user migration to Microsoft Teams. This migration is more simplified than path 1 because users are already using Skype for Business Online cloud services.

Gather a participant list for pilot testing, and then move users to Microsoft Teams. Ask all pilot participants to test all scenarios and then gather feedback. Use this feedback to make decisions about the actual business user migration.

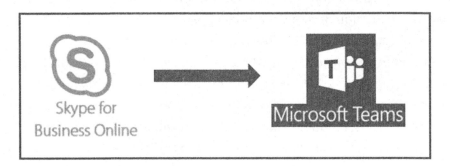

Figure 5-7. *Migration paths from Skype for Business Online to Microsoft Teams*

If your organization cannot move to Microsoft Teams because of a feature deficiency, it can start using Teams side by side with its existing unified communications (UC) solution such as Skype for Business. (See the sidebar, "Microsoft Teams Side by Side with Skype for Business.")

Table 5-2. *Microsoft Teams Available and Upcoming Features*

Microsoft Teams Available Features (March 2018)	Upcoming Features
Persistent 1:1 and Group Conversations	Contact Groups
Team + Channels for Teams Productivity	Unified Presence
Teams-SfB 1:1 Chat Interop	Federated Chat Between Teams and Skype for Business
Guest Access for External Users	Import Contacts from Skype for Business
Messaging Tenant-Level Policies	Skype for Business Interop with Persistent Chat
eDiscovery/Hold/Archiving of Messages	Messaging User-Level Policies
Schedule in Outlook and Teams	Message Retention Policies
Private and Channel Meetings	Broadcast Meetings
User-Facing Diagnostics	Cloud Recording
80 Users in a Meeting	Federated Meetings
Meeting Participant Management	Large Meeting Support (~250)
Audio Conferencing in over 90 Countries	Lobby for PSTN Callers
Anonymous Join	Outlook Meeting Schedule from Other Platforms (OWA, OLK, Mobile)
Enable Meeting Lifecycle with Pre/During/Post	PSTN Fallback
Desktop and Application Sharing	PowerPoint Load and Share
Conversations	Whiteboard and Meeting Notes
Give and Take Control in Sharing	Enable VTC Interop Services

(*continued*)

Table 5-2. (*continued*)

Microsoft Teams Available Features (March 2018)	Upcoming Features
Call Quality Diagnostic Portal	Skype Room Systems Support—Depends on Third Party
Tenant Policies	Surface Hub Support
Blind Transfer	Trio 1 Touch Teams Meeting Join—Depends on Third Party
Call Blocking	User-Level Meeting Policy
Call Forwarding	eDiscovery Enhancements
Caller ID and Masking	1:1 to Group Call Escalation with Teams, Skype for Business, and PSTN Participants
Call Hold	Boss and Delegate Support
e911 Support	Call Queues and Consultative Transfer
Enable Existing Calling Plan Support	Organizational Auto-Attendant
Extension Dialing	Distinctive Ring
Multi-call Handling	Forward to Group
Safe Transfer	Hybrid Connection to Teams
Simultaneous Ringing	Out-of-Office Support
Speed Dial	Call Support Between Teams and Skype Consumer
Suggested Contacts	Support for Existing Certified SIP Phones*
Transfer to PSTN Call	USB HID
Translate User Input to Standard Phone Format	eDiscovery Enhancements

(*continued*)

Table 5-2. (*continued*)

Microsoft Teams Available Features (March 2018)	Upcoming Features
Voicemail	Call Park and Group Call Pickup
SfB-Teams Calling—InterOp Support	Location-Based Routing
Windows, Mac, Edge, iOS, Android—Platform Support	Shared Line Appearance

MICROSOFT TEAMS SIDE BY SIDE WITH SKYPE FOR BUSINESS

Microsoft Teams is a native cloud-only solution, and there is no on-premises server available. In addition, currently Microsoft Teams does not have each and every feature that Skype for Business has. So, organizations should look the Microsoft Teams features available in Table 5-2 and then decide whether Microsoft Teams can meet their business requirements with the available features. If features are not there to fulfill the business needs, the organization can at least start adopting Microsoft Teams as a collaboration client, so that their users can get used to working with Microsoft Teams, because Microsoft Teams is going to be a single communications and collaboration solution eventually.

There are two options for using Microsoft Teams and Skype for Business side by side: managed and unmanaged.

Option 1: Unmanaged Side-by-Side Experience

This option, illustrated in Figure 5-8, is for organizations that do not want to control the Microsoft Teams and Skype for Business experience. In this option, users will be making the choice about their preferred communication client.

213

In this option, users initially start using Skype for Business and Microsoft Teams as two coexisting services. Both Skype for Business and Microsoft Teams clients will be installed on users' workstations and used for one-on-one and group chats, scheduled and ad hoc meetings, and calls including audio/video/ application sharing. When all features become available in Microsoft Teams, then as end-user Microsoft Teams will be the only client use for persistent chat, presence, meetings, calling, and collaboration needs.

Teams supports interoperability with Skype for Business Online users, and users will be given an opportunity to choose their preferred chat and calling app when they launch Teams. If one user picks Teams as the preferred app, and another user hasn't installed Teams or has picked Skype for Business as the preferred chat and calling app, they can continue to chat and call each other through the interop capabilities that are part of Microsoft Teams.

In this unmanaged side-by-side customer journey, prepare your help-desk team to handle support calls from users when facing issues with interop capabilities. Or advise users when to choose Teams meetings over Skype for Business meetings, and vice versa.

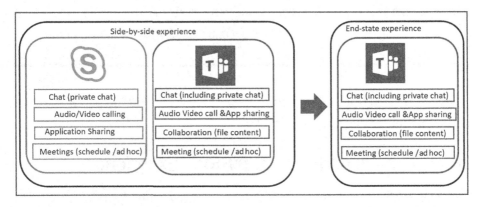

Figure 5-8. *Microsoft Teams and Skype for Business can coexist side by side*

Option 2: Managed Microsoft Teams and Skype for Business Client Side-by-Side Experience

There are multiple benefits of using Microsoft Teams and Skype for Business side by side.

This second option provides more control, because the organization administrator or support teams can control the Microsoft Teams and Skype for Business client experience by using a preferred client for communications. Using this option, support teams can introduce Microsoft Teams as the preferred client for chat and files, and later add meeting and collaboration options, and finally include the entire workload, including calling and application sharing.

Organizations that have Skype for Business as the only communication solution for chat (group chat and private chat), audio/video/PSTN calling and meeting (scheduled and ad hoc) then introduce Microsoft Teams as collaboration and private chat as side-by-side with Skype for Business. Default experience for user will be chat via Skype for Business and allowed chat between Skype for Business and Microsoft Teams, for meetings and calling use Skype for Business and collaboration purpose use Microsoft Teams.

There is no requirement to use either Skype for Business or Microsoft Teams exclusively for your chat conversations. As more of your coworkers begin using Teams, you should begin using Microsoft Teams as your primary chat client as well. And you should use Teams not only for chat, but also to help you connect more quickly with the people with whom you wish to collaborate. Figure 5-9 depicts this transition. In addition, by using Teams, you will have your conversation history available and the ability to load relevant files into the conversation, simplifying the conversation and speeding up the time it takes to find the relevant information.

You can use Microsoft Teams for an effective chat experience, as follows:

- Send a chat to any contact in your Outlook contact list, even when they are offline.

- Initiate and participate in group conversations to quickly share ideas and drive conversation.

- Use chat as a persistent experience.

- Insert memes and Giphy files, making communication fun and interactive.

- Capture and share an image with contacts quickly for simplified sharing of visuals.

- Access persistent chat conversation history to easily pick up a conversation at any time.

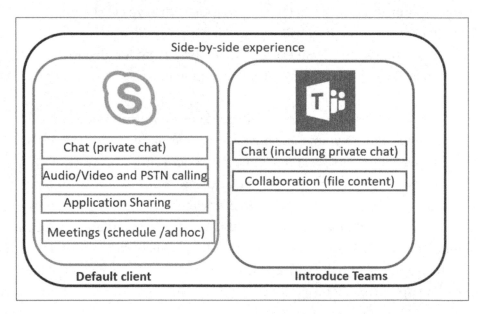

Figure 5-9. *Introduce Teams as a side-by-side option*

As next step, introduce Microsoft Teams for meetings along with chat and collaboration features, as shown in Figure 5-10. Continue to use Skype for Business for chat and audio/video calls, PSTN calls, and application-sharing features. Slowly stop using meetings through Skype for Business.

As you proceed with this Microsoft Teams journey, you can begin hosting your online meetings in Microsoft Teams. As one of the key ways for you to collaborate with your coworkers, creating and hosting a meeting in Teams gives you a single location to keep everything related to the conversation. Use teams and channels that you have already created for the meeting, and access content relevant to the discussion directly from the Teams interface. Microsoft Teams will slowly become your default client for meetings, including scheduled and ad hoc meetings.

There are multiple things you can do with Microsoft Teams for meetings:

- Schedule one-time or recurring meetings.

- Invite your coworkers and external partners or customers to a meeting.

- Share and collaborate during your meeting.

- Add others to your meeting on-the-fly in a channel.

- Store meeting presentations and Office files in one place, facilitating content reviews, and making meetings more productive

- Conduct meetings across devices with a consistent interface and experience

- Integrate with third-party apps

Before rolling out meetings in Microsoft Teams, do a complete test. The meeting can be scheduled via the Teams desktop client, a browser, or via Microsoft Outlook using the meeting add-in for Microsoft Teams.

After you've enabled scheduled meetings in Teams, first start educating users about creating new Teams meetings or updating existing Skype for Business meetings to Teams meetings.

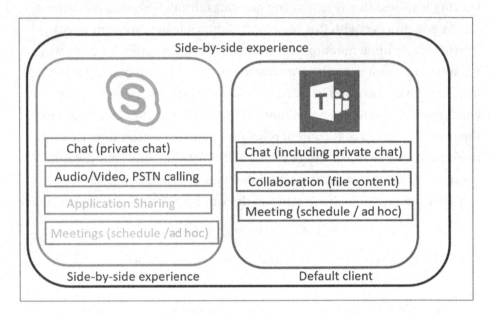

Figure 5-10. *Start adding Teams meetings to the side-by-side approach*

As the next step, introduce Microsoft Teams as the default client for calls—along with chat (group and private), meetings (scheduled and ad hoc), and collaboration (file content) features. Skype for Business will be there in silent mode.

As depicted in Figure 5-11, audio/video calls, PSTN calls, and application sharing are shifted from Skype for Business to Microsoft Teams, which becomes the default.

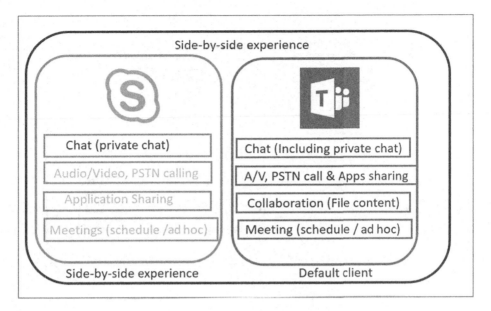

Figure 5-11. *Shift calling features to Microsoft Teams as you continue the side-by-side experience*

Before the rollout of audio/video calls, application sharing, and PSTN calls in Microsoft Teams, do a complete test; make private audio/video calls, and test PSTN inbound and outbound calls.

Finally, Microsoft Teams will be the only client available for chat (group chat and private chat with persistent experience), audio/video calls, PSTN calls, audio conferencing, meetings (scheduled/ad hoc), application/desktop sharing and collaboration features with file and application integration.

As shown in Figure 5-12, chat (including private chat), audio/video calls, PSTN calls, application sharing, meetings (scheduled and ad hoc) have shifted to Microsoft Teams as the default experience and away from the Skype for Business client.

Test all features—audio/video calls, application sharing, PSTN calls, meetings (scheduled/ad hoc)—in Microsoft Teams before the rollout.

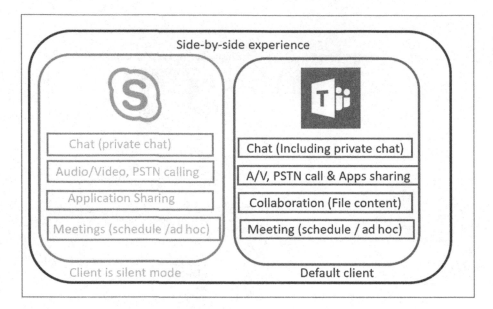

Figure 5-12. *Make Teams the default client, and Skype for Business is in silent mode*

Piloting Teams Alongside Skype for Business

After you optimize your existing environment for real-time communication, the next step is to enable Microsoft Teams for your organization on the Office 365 tenant and configure it correctly.

Refer to Chapter 2 for details on enabling the various options of Microsoft Teams. When Microsoft Teams is ready for use, the next step is to start piloting Microsoft Teams. This section will help you understand the piloting process.

Piloting is testing or validating functionality with a minimal number of users. Starting a pilot is the first step to allowing your users to use or test a Microsoft Teams workload. Running a successful pilot is important because your eventual decision to move forward with Microsoft Teams is dependent on the successful outcome of the pilot.

Microsoft Teams Pilot

Reach out across a few departments to identify one or two pilot teams. In order to participate in the pilot, the entire team should commit to using Microsoft Teams as its primary way to communicate with each other and to collaborate on projects for at least 1 week to 30 days. This gives pilot teams the opportunity to fully understand the capabilities of Microsoft Teams, and to identify the best ways to integrate it into their workflows.

Figure 5-13 shows Teams pilot plan.

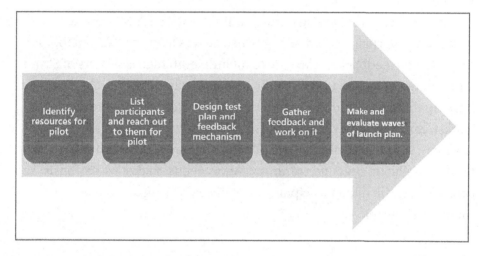

Figure 5-13. *Pilot plan*

Identify your resources for the pilot. For example, identify the set of users who can use Microsoft Teams capabilities for day-to-day use and can provide feedback. Then set a timeline for the pilot and create an articulated test plan.

Once you identify the pilot participants, look for business scenarios and use cases that can be used in the test plan. Review your current usage reports for Skype for Business and/or conduct a focus group with your top Skype for Business users to better understand their current collaboration and communication scenarios.

For the pilot, you must define a clear start and end date to maintain momentum and allow time to assess the impact. A minimum 30-day pilot is recommended. Start with small group and add to your pilot group as appropriate—whether additional workloads/features or additional users, making time to assess results and adjust your pilot as you iterate.

Also, setting clear goals will provide a mechanism you can use to measure success and define your best path forward. Sample goals and success criteria are provided in Pilot Essentials Resources by Microsoft. You can download these resources at `https://go.microsoft.com/fwlink/?linkid=859067`.

Identifying and selecting participants for your pilot is important because the participants are going to use Teams features and capabilities and give you feedback. Make sure to include both high-adopters of Skype for Business as well as users/groups who would benefit from the teamwork hub capabilities of Teams. Consider using a current cross-team project workstream for pilot user selection as well as a realistic use case for your test plan. Also make sure that the pilot participants use Microsoft Teams for their collaboration and communication needs on day-to-day basis. You can separate the pilot participants into different groups and reach out to them for feedback.

Test Plan

A successful pilot experience provides your participants with clearly defined tasks to complete, along with a feedback loop. Group tasks together to present real-world scenarios to your users, demonstrating relevancy to their daily activities. Your organization may opt to pilot all functionality at once, or leverage a gradual approach (for example, first pilot collaboration, then meetings, then chat and calling). Ensure that you have an open feedback channel to track progress and measure outcomes. A predefined survey is an easy way to capture and assess pilot results and should be designed based on the scenarios and features in your test plan.

Before starting the pilot, participants should do the following:

- Install the Teams desktop client

- Install the Teams mobile client

- Set preferences to make Microsoft Teams their default client for chat, group chat, calling, and meeting

- View available Teams training to become familiar with how to use Teams

- Become familiar with T-Bot in order to ask questions about Teams functionality

In the tests, use Microsoft Teams for daily interaction, including one-to-one chats and group chats, one-to-one calls, and internal meetings. Here is a list of features they can test and use:

- Initiate a chat (whether the recipient is offline or online)

- Add multiple users to a chat and have a conversation

- Add audio/video to an IM

- Add app share to an IM

- Add another contact to an IM

- Add a meme/Giphy file to an IM

- Attach a file to an IM

- Search for a contact

- Call a contact

- Whenever possible, connect Microsoft Teams on mobile devices and test similar features.

You should also test Microsoft Teams meeting capabilities whenever possible. Here are some sample tests related to meetings:

- Schedule a meeting in Outlook

- Schedule a meeting in Teams

- Send a file in advance of the meeting

- Live app share during the meeting

- Take questions during the meeting

Finally, test collaboration features using Microsoft Teams. The following are tasks to test:

- Create a new team

- Invite users to a team

- Create new channels within the team, and then invite users

- Communicate updates and questions via conversations in respective channels

- Mention an @user alias to call out their call-to-action

- Post and link to files within the team

- Schedule and host a meeting within the channel or team to discuss the project's status

Frequently communicating with pilot teams is another important task. Educating pilot participants about what is happening, when, and why, as well as what is expected of them, is crucial to the success of your pilot. In addition, you should send communications that include links to training and support so users can get additional information as they progress through the pilot.

Here are links to Microsoft Teams user-level training videos:

- https://support.office.com/article/Office-Training-Center-b8f02f81-ec85-4493-a39b-4c48e6bc4bfb

- https://support.office.com/teams

Evaluation for Go-Forward Plan

Evaluation of Teams depends on your pilot's feedback and results. After the pilot is completed, gather all feedback surveys, user counts and inputs, final network stats, and support tickets for analysis against your pilot goals and determination of your plan forward. Based on all outcomes, here are a few recommended paths your organization may take as you continue your journey from Skype for Business to Microsoft Teams:

1. Use Microsoft Teams and Skype for Business Online side by side.

2. Use Microsoft Teams and Skype for Business on-premises side by side.

3. Plan for the actual migration.

4. Use Direct route for Phone system

Driving Microsoft Teams User Adoption

Driving the user adoption of Microsoft Teams is another important step, because until users use Teams, they cannot realize the value and benefits that it provides. Promoting adoption is continuous work. As your organization's administrator or support person, you might be dealing with users who don't like change unless they can see the benefits and value. That's why user adoption is a very important phase.

As I mentioned earlier, Microsoft Teams is the hub for teamwork in Office 365, which brings a lot of features such as chat, calls and meetings, file content, easy integration with Office 365 apps, and flexible security and governance for each team. In order to use all these features, the user must be aware of this functionality and how to use it.

As part of the adoption process, be sure to make available all training resources, documentation, and frequently asked questions. Make sure your users get answers to their queries.

In addition, identify the early adopters and enthusiastic users who are always ready for change. These are the people who will be willing to test Microsoft Teams capabilities and submit feedback. Be sure to measure these changes, because without measurement criteria, you cannot justify the feedback you get. IT partners are other early adopters who are always ready for testing. So include both as early adopters and make proper plans and test cases to use.

Read the following to facilitate user adoption:

- Microsoft Teams journey frequently asked questions: `https://docs.microsoft.com/en-us/MicrosoftTeams/faq-journey`

- Help URL: `https://support.office.com/teams`

You also should make available user training resources. Share Teams training resources to improve the learning curve. Microsoft has a user training video, and you can share its link with your users so they can learn how to use each feature. The following are links for training resources:

- Office 365 Training URL: `https://support.office.com/article/Office-Training-Center-b8f02f81-ec85-4493-a39b-4c48e6bc4bfb`

- Microsoft Teams Training Video URLs: `https://support.office.com/en-us/article/microsoft-teams-video-training-4f108e54-240b-4351-8084-b1089f0d21d7?wt.mc_id=otc_home&ui=en-US&rs=en-US&ad=US`

Finally, create and distribute how-to documents. You can write step-by-step process documents and share them with users. In addition, create common use cases to share with your users. You can provide Teams Help topics for users to accelerate their onboarding. Leverage the Office 365 Adoption Guide (`https://go.microsoft.com/fwlink/?linkid=859045`).

Microsoft Teams Chat/Conversations

Using chat is one of the most effective ways to reach out to your coworkers. Sending a quick chat is an easy and fast way to become familiar with Microsoft Teams. Users can send a chat to single contact or start a group conversation. With the chat history included in the conversation, they can easily reference previous conversations with the person or groups.

Here is list of things you can do with Microsoft Teams chat:

- Send an IM to any contact in your Outlook contact list, even when they are offline.

- Initiate and participate in group conversations to quickly share ideas and drive conversations.

- Insert memes and Giphy files, making communication fun and interactive.

- Capture and share an image with contacts quickly for simplified sharing of visuals.

- Access persistent conversation history to easily pick up a conversation at any time.

Microsoft Teams Meeting

Encourage your users to use Microsoft Teams meetings. For meetings with other teams in your organization, especially those that already share teams and channels, this is a terrific way to extend users collaboration and link the meeting, persistent chat, conversations, and supporting documents together. Users can schedule team meetings by using the Meetings tab or through the Teams Outlook add-in.

If you have meetings with external contacts, or recurring meetings that are currently scheduled in Skype for Business, there is no need to reschedule those meetings at this time.

Here is the list of tasks users can do with a Microsoft Teams meeting:

- Schedule one-time or recurring meetings.

- Share and collaborate during your meeting.

- Add others to your meeting on-the-fly.

- Store Office files in one place, facilitating content reviews and making meetings more productive.

- Conduct meetings across devices with a consistent interface and experience.

- Integrate with third-party apps.

Microsoft Teams Calling

Motivate users to use Microsoft Teams for one-to-one audio/video calls, application sharing, and more.

Here is the list of tasks users can do with Microsoft Teams calling:

- Call one-to-one using audio/video.

- Use application sharing during the call.

- Call to an outbound PSTN number and receive an inbound call from a PSTN number.

Microsoft Teams Roadmap

Table 5-3 provides the complete Microsoft Teams roadmap for messaging, meeting, and calling capabilities at the time of this writing (March 2018). For the latest roadmap, refer to `https://go.microsoft.com/fwlink/?linkid=859047`.

Table 5-3. *Teams Roadmap*

Feature Grade	Feature Available as of Feb 2018	Coming in 1Q CY2018 (End of Qtr)	Coming in 4Q CY2018
Messaging Roadmap			
Enterprise grade	✓ Persistent 1:1 and Group Conversations	Share/Mute Chat	
	✓ Team + Channels for Teams Productivity		
	✓ Hide Chat		

(*continued*)

Table 5-3. (*continued*)

Feature Grade	Feature Available as of Feb 2018	Coming in 1Q CY2018 (End of Qtr)	Coming in 4Q CY2018
Skype for Business interop and federation	✓ Teams-SfB 1:1 Chat Interop	• Contact Groups	
	✓ Guest Access for External Users	• Unified Presence	
		• Federated Chat Between Teams and Skype for Business	
		• Import Contacts from Skype for Business	
		• Skype for Business Interop with Persistent Chat	
Platform and devices	Windows, Mac, Edge, Chrome iOS, Android, Windows Phone		
IT Pro	✓ Messaging Tenant-Level policies	• Messaging User-Level Policies	
	✓ eDiscovery/Hold/ Archiving of Messages	• Message Retention Policies	
	✓ Messaging Interop IT Policies		

(*continued*)

Table 5-3. (*continued*)

Feature Grade	Feature Available as of Feb 2018	Coming in 1Q CY2018 (End of Qtr)	Coming in 4Q CY2018
	Meetings Roadmap		
Enterprise grade	✓ Schedule in Outlook & Teams	• Broadcast Meetings	
	✓ Private and Channel Meetings	• Cloud Recording	
	✓ User-Facing Diagnostics	• Federated Meetings	
	✓ 80 Users in a Meeting	• Large Meeting Support (~250)	
	✓ Audio Conferencing (Preview)	• Lobby for PSTN Callers	
	✓ Participant Management	• Outlook Meeting Schedule from other Platforms (OWA, OLK, Mobile)	
	✓ Improved Device Selection	• PSTN Fallback	
	✓ Audio Conferencing in over 90 Countries		
	✓ Anonymous Join		
	✓ Interactive Troubleshooting		

(*continued*)

Table 5-3. (*continued*)

Feature Grade	Feature Available as of Feb 2018	Coming in 1Q CY2018 (End of Qtr)	Coming in 4Q CY2018
	✓ Lobby Support		
	✓ Mute Other Participant		
Collaborative meetings	✓ Enable Meeting Lifecycle with Pre/ During/Post	• PowerPoint Load and Share	
	✓ Desktop Sharing	• Whiteboard and Meeting Notes	
	✓ Conversations		
	✓ Immersive Meeting Experiences		
	✓ Application Sharing		
	✓ Give and Take Control in Sharing		
Platform and devices	✓ Windows, Mac	• Enable VTC Interop Services*	
	✓ Mobile: iOS and Android Meetings	• Skype Room Systems Support*	
	✓ Edge, Chrome Browser Support for Meetings	• Surface Hub Support	

(*continued*)

Table 5-3. (*continued*)

Feature Grade	Feature Available as of Feb 2018	Coming in 1Q CY2018 (End of Qtr)	Coming in 4Q CY2018
		• Trio 1 Touch Teams Meeting Join*	
IT Pro	✓ Call Quality Diagnostic Portal	• User-Level Meeting Policy	
	✓ Tenant Policies	• eDiscovery Enhancements	
	✓ Enable Call Quality Analytics		

Calling Roadmap

Feature Grade	Feature Available as of Feb 2018	Coming in 1Q CY2018 (End of Qtr)	Coming in 4Q CY2018
Enterprise grade	✓ Blind Transfer / Call Blocking / Call Forwarding	• 1:1 to Group Call Escalation with Teams, Skype for Business, and PSTN participants	• Call Park
	✓ Caller ID Masking / e911 Support	• Boss and Delegate Support / Call Queues	• Location-Based Routing
	✓ Enable Existing Calling Plan Support	• Consultative Transfer / Organizational Auto-Attendant	• Shared Line Appearance
	✓ Extension Dialing / Hold / Voicemail	• Do Not Disturb Breakthrough	• Group Call Pickup

(continued)

Table 5-3. (*continued*)

Feature Grade	Feature Available as of Feb 2018	Coming in 1Q CY2018 (End of Qtr)	Coming in 4Q CY2018
	✓ Multicall Handling / Safe Transfer	• Distinctive Ring / Forward to Group	
	✓ Simultaneous Ringing / Speed Dial	• Hybrid Connection to Teams	
	✓ Suggested Contacts / Transfer to PSTN Call	• Out-of-Office Support	
	✓ Translate User Input to Standard Phone Format		
Skype for Business interop & fed	✓ SfB-Teams Calling	• Call Support Between Teams & Skype Consumer	
Platform and devices	✓ TTY Support	• Support for Existing Certified SIP Phones*	
	✓ Windows, Mac, Edge, iOS, Android	• USB HID	
IT Pro	✓ Call Quality Diagnostic Portal	• eDiscovery Enhancements	
	✓ SfB-Teams Interop Policies		

* Capability has third-party dependencies

Summary

This chapter covered the journey from Skype for Business to Microsoft Teams. To start this journey, organizations should optimize their existing Skype for Business server environment, which will be used by Teams. Moving from Skype for Business to Microsoft Teams is not a straightforward migration, because Microsoft Teams is a cloud-only solution, whereas Skype for Business is available for the cloud and on-premises. I recommend using Microsoft Teams and Skype for Business side by side for now, because at this time Microsoft Teams does not have every feature that Skype for Business has. Using both will meet organizations' needs. As you learned in this chapter, piloting Microsoft Teams alongside Skype for Business is another important step. In addition, encouraging users to adopt Microsoft Teams is as important as piloting Teams. At the end of the chapter, you learned about the Microsoft Teams detailed roadmap.

CHAPTER 6

Microsoft Teams Troubleshooting

In this chapter, you'll learn about Microsoft Teams client settings, tips and best practices, and end-to-end troubleshooting using diagnostic logs and common troubleshooting scenarios. This chapter covers the following topics:

- Understanding Microsoft Teams basic troubleshooting

- Gathering Teams diagnostic logs and analysis

- Microsoft Teams common troubleshooting scenarios

- Tips and tricks for Microsoft Teams

- Microsoft Teams and Skype for Business Admin Center tool

- Microsoft Teams monitoring, reporting, and analytics

- Auditing for a Microsoft Teams event

© Balu N Ilag 2018
B.N. Ilag, *Introducing Microsoft Teams*, https://doi.org/10.1007/978-1-4842-3567-6_6

Understanding Microsoft Teams Basic Troubleshooting

Understanding Microsoft Teams is first step for troubleshooting, Teams is cloud-only service means troubleshooting is divided in to two part service level troubleshooting which is taken care by Microsoft and second is Teams client level troubleshooting which is done Teams administrator.

Microsoft Teams is purely a cloud-only service. No back-end infrastructure is on premises, so the administrator's responsibilities have changed toward troubleshooting. Microsoft, as a service provider, takes care of Microsoft Teams cloud-service-level problems. But as a support administrator, your responsibilities are still there to plan and prepare your environment, support end-user problems and dependency/compatibility problems, and optimize your organization's network to use Microsoft Teams effectively.

As I mentioned earlier, Microsoft Teams is collaboration hub with multiple capabilities, and these capabilities come from different services. Therefore, Teams is dependent on different services for different capabilities, such as Office 365 groups, SharePoint Online, Skype for Business Online, and the Skype infrastructure. This dependency makes Teams more complex. In addition, Teams has clients for all platforms, including, Windows, macOS, iOS, Android, and web clients.

Microsoft Teams uses a User Principal Name to sign in (for example, bilag@mydomin.com). Its back-end microservices architecture doesn't have any dependency on the SIP URI as Skype for Business has. The Microsoft Teams client has a new user interface that is built with Electron as a wrapper and Chromium as its core. This client is self-updating, so there is no need to update it manually or through System Center Configuration Manager (SCCM).

Because Microsoft Teams is a cloud-only service that's part of the Office 365 suite, there is not much you can do from the back end. This means there is very little debugging you can do for Teams services. However, you can do more troubleshooting on the Microsoft Teams client side; you can check and analyze call-quality issues, call-setup failure, service-degradation issues, sign-in issues, and more. This chapter provides complete information on troubleshooting Teams issues and will show you different aspects of troubleshooting.

Before spending time investigating an issue, check service health. Service health for Microsoft Teams is displayed on the Office 365 Admin portal main page. Before troubleshooting issues with the client, it is good practice to verify that the Teams service is healthy and to look for any service degradation alerts. Figure 6-1 shows the page for Service Health. On this page, you can check for alerts about any service outages and for any open support tickets, for example.

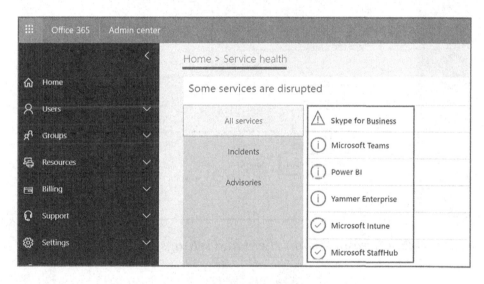

Figure 6-1. *Microsoft Teams Service Health page*

Microsoft Teams Client Settings

You need to understand Teams applications and settings before you can attempt core troubleshooting. There are many things you can do with the Teams client: change a profile picture, change notification settings, find keyboard shortcuts, check Teams apps versions and updates, and more.

It is easy to see or change Teams settings. Click your profile picture on the left side of the Teams app, and you can see all available settings, as shown in Figure 6-2.

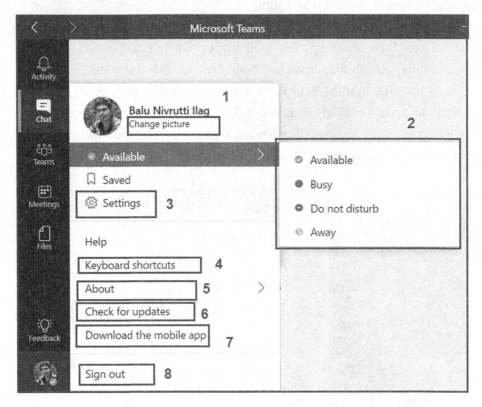

Figure 6-2.   *Microsoft Teams client and settings*

You can make the following settings changes:

- Change your picture.

- Set your status (there are four statuses available).

- Change application settings and notifications.

- Find keyboard shortcuts.

- Find out which version of Teams you're on (click About ➤ Version).

- Check for updates. Your desktop app automatically updates (so you don't have to). If you want, you can still check for available updates by clicking Check for Updates. You will see the message "Your web app is always up-to-date."

- Get a link to download the mobile app.

- Sign out from the application.

Sending Feedback

If you want to tell Microsoft what you think about Microsoft Teams, you can provide feedback. Simply click Feedback at the bottom-left corner of your screen, as shown in Figure 6-3.

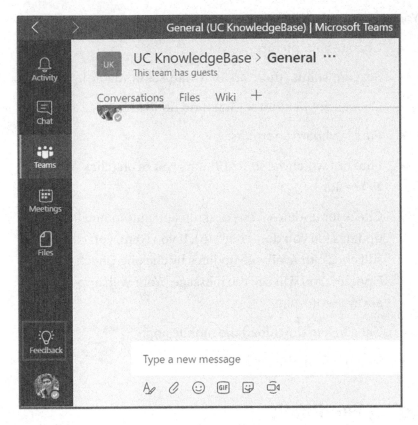

Figure 6-3. *The Feedback option in Teams*

Refreshing Microsoft Teams to Show Current Information

If there is an issue with the Microsoft Teams application, you can click the Refresh Now button in the Teams application, shown in Figure 6-4.

Figure 6-4. *Refreshing the Teams client*

Starting or Quitting the Teams Client

You can manually restart the Teams app by right-clicking the Teams icon in your dock (Mac) or taskbar (Windows) and selecting Quit (see Figure 6-5).

Figure 6-5. *Quitting the Teams app*

After you quit, you can reopen Teams apps by searching Teams or clicking the Teams icon.

Recovering from a Teams App Crash

If the Teams app crashes when you use conversation or call functionality, you can uninstall the Teams app and reinstall it again. Directions for Windows and Mac computers follows.

For Windows

To uninstall the app in Windows, follow these steps:

1. Choose Start ➤ Control Panel ➤ Programs and Features.

2. Click the Microsoft Teams option. Then click the Uninstall option, shown in Figure 6-6. Complete the uninstallation.

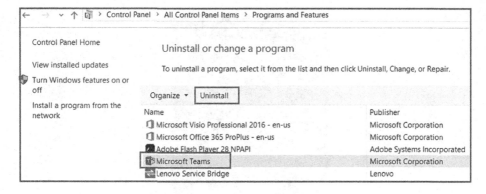

Figure 6-6. Uninstalling Teams

3. Restart your computer after the Teams app uninstallation.

4. Visit the Teams site to download and install the Teams app (`https://teams.microsoft.com`). Log in to Teams and then download and install the Microsoft Teams app.

For Mac

Quit Teams by right-clicking the Teams app in the dock, and then holding down Option and clicking Force Quit. Open the Application folder, select Microsoft Teams, and move it to the Trash.

Microsoft Teams Mobile Client Troubleshooting

Microsoft is continually investing in the Teams mobile app to enhance the user experience and adding new capabilities to it. So, it is a best practice to be on the latest Teams app version. Always check your Teams app version to make sure it's up-to-date.

Here is the basic troubleshooting you should do with the Microsoft Teams mobile app:

1. Download the Microsoft Teams app on your iOS mobile device from the App Store and install it.

2. Once the Teams apps is installed, open it and type your User Principal Name (for example, bilag@ mydpmain.com); this is similar to your e-mail address. Then click Sign In, as shown in Figure 6-7.

Figure 6-7. *Teams mobile app*

  3. To check Teams mobile app settings, tap More and
      then Settings.

Under Settings, there are many things that you can do, as shown in
Figure 6-8.

Figure 6-8. *Teams mobile app settings*

The mobile app settings are as follows:

- *Notifications*: You can turn notifications on or off for different workloads such as chats, mentions, missed calls, and voicemail.

- *Options*: With this setting, you can turn on or off various options including Show History, Clear History, Clear Downloaded Files, and Clear App Data.

- *Send feedback*: You use this option to submit feedback to the Microsoft Teams product team.

- *Help*: Here you can ask T-Bot to help or see Help articles.

- *About*: Here you can see Teams version details.

- *Report an issue*: You can use this option when you want to report an issue and send logs.

- *Sign out*: You can use this option to sign out from Teams.

Signing in to Microsoft Teams

Because many users are new to Microsoft Teams, a common question is, How do I sign-in to Teams? That concern has lead me to discuss sign-in issues and troubleshooting here.

To sign in to Teams, you need an Office 365 account with the appropriate Office 365 license plan (for example, `bilag@mydomain.com`).

The following license plans support Microsoft Teams:

- Business Essentials

- Business Premium

- Office 365 F1

- Enterprise E1, E3, or E5

- Enterprise E4 (for anyone who purchased this plan prior to its retirement)

- Office 365 Education

- Office 365 Education Plus

- Office 365 Education E5, as well as existing Office 365 Education E3 customers who purchased E3 prior to its retirement

Microsoft Teams isn't available for Government tenants.

Microsoft Teams uses Modern Authentication for signing in. Modern Authentication means single sign-on (SSO). The advantage of using Modern Authentication is that it makes it possible for you to sign in to Microsoft Teams without re-entering your UPN or e-mail and password every time you want to start a new session. It's a more secure and reliable way to sign in to Microsoft Teams.

Understanding Modern Authentication

Modern Authentication is a process that allows you to sign in to an application securely, without a lengthy process. Because Modern Authentication includes SSO, it's also part of the process that lets Microsoft Teams know that you have already entered your credentials (for example, your work e-mail and password) elsewhere, such as in the Office 365 portal, and you shouldn't be required to enter them again to launch the Teams app.

Modern Authentication is hardwired into Microsoft Teams, and it should be able to recognize your credentials as linked to your Office 365 account.

If your company enabled Multifactor Authentication (MFA), you have to verify your credential via your phone, by providing a unique code or entering a PIN number or presenting your thumbprint. For Single-Factor Authentication, you won't be required to provide your credentials again for Teams, Microsoft Teams will automatically sign in to your account after you launch the app from the same machine where enter your credentials for the other application.

Signing in to Teams Mobile Apps

Microsoft Teams uses single sign-on through Active Directory on your mobile device. There is one sign-in for Teams and your other Office 365 apps, and you won't need to reenter your credentials when you launch Teams or your Office 365 apps from the same device.

If your organization has multifactor authentication set up, there can be an additional step and level of security associated with your sign-in. For example, after you enter your credentials, you might be asked to verify your sign-in via a phone call by providing a unique code, your thumbprint, or a PIN number.

If you get an error message while signing in to teams, there might be something wrong with your domain or your company's Office 365 account. Your IT administrator will be your point contact in terms of resolving the sign-in issue.

In many cases, only your IT admin or system admin will be able to resolve the issue for you. So, after trying the basic troubleshooting suggestions in Table 6-1, contact them with the status code in this table.

Table 6-1. *Sign-in Issues, Error Codes, and Troubleshooting Actions*

Code	Description	Troubleshooting Action
0xCAA20003	You ran into an authorization problem.	Make sure your date and time are set up correctly. Whether your date and time are accurate will affect your ability to connect to secure sites (HTTPS).
0xCAA82EE2	The request has timed out.	Ensure that you are connected to the Internet. Then work with your IT admin to ensure that other apps or a firewall configuration aren't preventing access.
0xCAA82EE7	The server name could not be resolved.	Ensure that you are connected to the Internet. Then work with your IT admin to ensure that other apps or a firewall configuration aren't preventing access.
0xCAA20004	Your request needs to be approved by a resource owner or authorization server.	Ask your IT admin to can confirm that your organization is complying with Azure Active Directory (AAD) configuration policies.
0xCAA90018	You're not using the right credentials.	The Windows credentials you signed in with are different from your Office 365 credentials. Try to sign in again with the correct e-mail/password combination. If you continue to receive this status code, contact your IT admin.
none	You'll need to reenter your PIN by using a smart card.	Reinsert your smart card. Also, your smart card certificate might be corrupt, in which case, contact your IT admin.

Gathering Teams Diagnostic Logs and Analysis

As administrators, we always deal with end-user problems. While troubleshooting, the most important thing that helps us are log files. Without diagnostic logs, you cannot do in-depth troubleshooting. That's why an important element of troubleshooting is capturing the right diagnostic logs from Microsoft Teams. Teams clients have rich logging capabilities that will assist in troubleshooting many end-user problems.

This section provides step-by-step information on collecting and analyzing logs for Microsoft Teams, from the following:

- Microsoft Teams Desktop and Mac Client Logs
- Microsoft Teams Mobile Client
- Microsoft Teams Web Client
- Reading Microsoft Teams Client Logs
- IP Address and Port Requirements

Microsoft Teams Desktop and Mac Client Logs

Microsoft Teams has three types of logs, which are stored in different locations:

- Web logs
- Desktop logs
- Media stack logs

To capture Teams diagnostics logs, follow the steps in each of the following subsections.

Web Logs

Web logs contain most of the Teams client activity. When you're troubleshooting, these logs are the best ones to start with.

Teams Windows Client

To capture logs from a Windows system:

1. Open Teams client then right-click the Microsoft
    Teams icon in your application tray, select Get Logs.
    You will see message like the following:

2. %downloads%\MSTeams Diagnostics Log
    <timestamp>.txt, as shown in Figure 6-9.

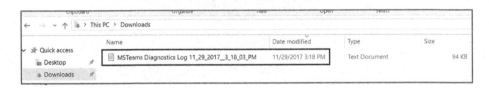

Figure 6-9. *Microsoft Teams logs*

Mac

To capture logs on a Mac system, here are the steps:

1. Press Command+Option+Shift+1 in the client to
    download the logs.

2. Downloads\MSTeams Diagnostics Log
    <timestamp>.txt

Desktop Logs

Desktop logs have the most information about the framework and
bootstrapping, the app bootstrap process, plug-in initialization, update
management, and SSO/ADAL sign-in.

- Windows: %appdata%\Microsoft\Teams\logs.txt (see Figure 6-10).

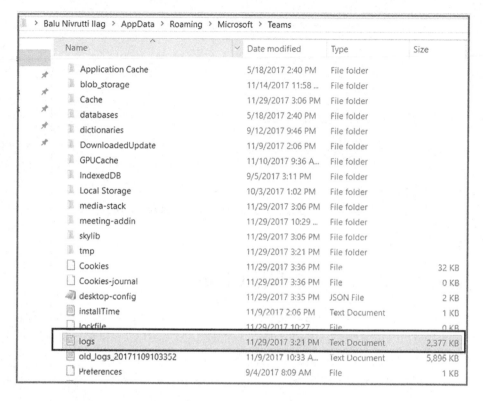

Figure 6-10.   Teams logs

- For Mac: `~/Library/Application Support/ Microsoft/Teams/logs.txt`

Media Stack Logs

Media stack logs have information related to media connectivity.

- For Windows, you can find these logs at `%appdata%\ Microsoft\Teams\media-stack` (see Figure 6-11).

Name	Date modified	Type	Size
Teams.msrtc.blog	11/29/2017 3:14 PM	BLOG File	18 KB
Teams.msrtc-1.blog	11/16/2017 7:46 PM	BLOG File	35 KB
Teams_MediaStack-6.2.6.802-local-amd64fre-U.etl	9/5/2017 3:34 PM	ETL File	168 KB
Teams_MediaStack-6.2.6.802-local-amd64fre-U.etl.bak	9/4/2017 8:09 AM	BAK File	240 KB
Teams_MediaStackETW.etl	10/24/2017 11:53 ...	ETL File	16 KB
Teams_MediaStackETW.etl.bak	10/13/2017 7:18 A...	BAK File	40 KB
Teams_MediaStackETW-6.0.8978.135-releases_CL2017_R03-amd6...	6/15/2017 12:14 PM	ETL File	32 KB
Teams_MediaStackETW-6.0.8978.135-releases_CL2017_R03-amd6...	6/14/2017 8:18 PM	BAK File	32 KB
Teams_MediaStackETW-6.2.12.623-UVA-X86CHK-U.etl	11/29/2017 3:06 PM	ETL File	0 KB
Teams_MediaStackETW-6.2.12.623-UVA-X86CHK-U.etl.bak	11/16/2017 8:16 PM	BAK File	24 KB

> Balu Nivrutti Ilag > AppData > Roaming > Microsoft > Teams > media-stack

Figure 6-11. *Teams Media stack logs*

- On a Mac, media stack logs are located at ~/Library/ Application Support/Microsoft/Teams/media-stack/*.*.

Microsoft Teams Mobile Client

When you are troubleshooting Teams mobile client issues, you should first restart the client. If the issue does not resolve, the next step is to collect Teams mobile client logs and analyze them to find the issue.

To collect Teams mobile client logs, follow these steps:

1. Open the Microsoft Teams app on your iOS device. Then click the client icon and then Settings.

2. Click the Report an Issue option, as shown in Figure 6-12.

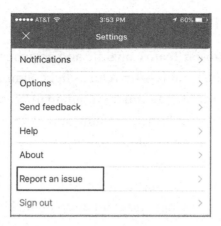

Figure 6-12. *Teams mobile app option for reporting an issue*

Your e-mail program will open with a `log.txt` attachment file, as shown in Figure 6-13. Send the log to Microsoft or any other e-mail address. (The default e-mail address is Microsoft's.)

Figure 6-13. *Teams mobile client log file*

Microsoft Teams Web Client

You can log in to Microsoft Teams anytime and anywhere by using any computer, without installing the Teams client. Simply browse to https://teams.microsoft.com and then sign in to Teams by using your organization-provided User Principal Name and password.

If you encounter any issues while signing in, or any other issues in the Teams web client, close the browser. Then open a new browser and browse to the Teams web URL again. If you still have issues, the next step is to gather Teams web client logs and send them to the IT support team for further analysis.

To gather the logs, you can browse to the Teams site (teams. microsoft.com) from any web browser. Press Ctrl+U to see the Page Source. Alternatively, you can right-click in the browser and select View Source. Then send this log to the support team.

Figure 6-14 shows an example log from the Edge browser.

Figure 6-14. *Teams web client log*

Reading Microsoft Teams Client Logs

In the Skype for Business world, we use the Snooper tool to open the Skype for Business UCCAPI log for sign-in and media connectivity issues. However, in the Microsoft Teams world, Snooper isn't required.

You can open a Teams client log in any text editor, such as Notepad. However, the log will not be shown in its proper format, because the Teams client log has JSON content. Using an application with a JSON format extension viewer is recommended for opening a Microsoft Teams log. Editors that can be useful for this purpose include Sublime, Chrome, and Visual Studio Code. My favorite is Sublime, and it works great

Troubleshooting Teams Client HTTPS Traffic

As I mentioned earlier, Teams uses HTTPS as a protocol for web traffic. When you are troubleshooting Teams client issues, it is a best practice to capture Teams HTTPS traffic and analyze it for any connectivity failures or service issues.

There are many traffic-capturing tools. However, Fiddler and Charles work great for Microsoft Teams HTTPS traffic.

Fiddler has the ability to filter by client processes, so we can see Teams-specific traffic and connections that will be helpful for troubleshooting.

Charles has two views, Structure and Sequence, as shown in Figure 6-15.

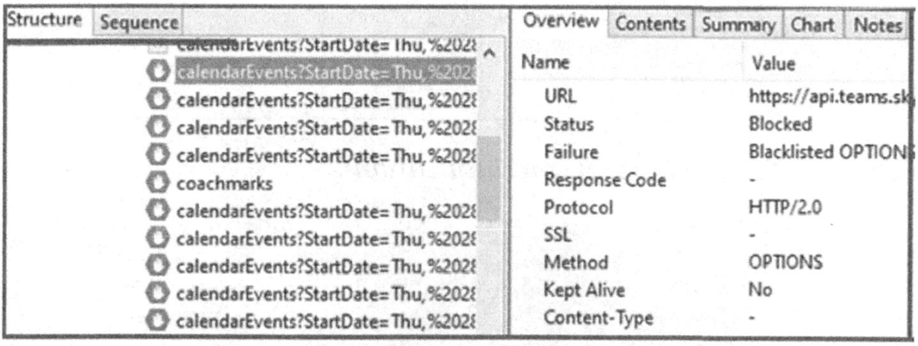

Figure 6-15.   Teams log analysis using Charles

The Structure view is helpful for seeing activity to specific service URLs.

To trace Teams traffic and responses, you need to decrypt the HTTPS traffic. This requires a root certificate from Fiddler or Charles that is installed in Trusted Root Certificate store in Personal or computer store in Microsoft Management Console (MMC).

Troubleshooting Teams Media Traffic

For media traffic troubleshooting, you must have client network traces. You can use any network monitoring tool to capture network traces, including NetMon (Network Monitor), Wireshark, or Message Analyzer.

My favorite is Wireshark, because you can filter traffic by source or destination IP address, protocol, source and destination port number, and so forth. This capability is beneficial for troubleshooting.

You can download Wireshark from www.wireshark.org/download.html.

If you want NetMon, you can download it from www.microsoft.com/ en-us/download/details.aspx?id=4865.

As an example, Figure 6-16 shows the media traffic for an audio/video call between two Teams clients. Teams client1 and Teams client2 are talking. Teams client1 is talking to Teams client2 over audio port 50006 <-> 50002.

14758 27.857459	Teams client1		Teams client2	UDP	147 50006 → 50002 Len=105
14759 27.861455	Teams client2		Teams client1	UDP	121 50002 → 50006 Len=79
14760 27.877900	Teams client1			UDP	145 50006 → 50002 Len=103
14761 27.881004	Teams client2		Teams client1	UDP	114 50002 → 50006 Len=72
14762 27.896742	Teams client1		Teams client2	UDP	165 50006 → 50002 Len=123
14763 27.900434	Teams client2		Teams client1	UDP	117 50002 → 50006 Len=75
14764 27.917401	Teams client1		Teams client2	UDP	163 50006 → 50002 Len=121
14765 27.920711	Teams client2		Teams client1	UDP	109 50002 → 50006 Len=67
14766 27.937765	Teams client1		Teams client1	UDP	151 50006 → 50002 Len=109
14767 27.940068	Teams client2		Teams client2	UDP	118 50002 → 50006 Len=76

Figure 6-16. Teams client communication

In this call, media is flowing between two Teams clients. However, most of the time, direct connectivity is not allowed, especially when both clients are behind the firewall. Then the Teams media will flow through a cloud transport relay. So, it is recommended to allow UDP ports 3478 to 3481 for media, and to fall back to TCP port 443 when UDP is not available. The call quality will be better over UDP, as compared to TCP.

Most connectivity and call failure issues occur because of firewalls that may block traffic. Make sure that all required URLs, IP addresses, and ports are opened in the firewall or proxy.

IP Address and Port Requirements

The Microsoft Teams media workload uses specific ports and URLs. Organizations must verify that the necessary URLs, IP addresses, and ports are opened in their firewall or proxy in order to minimize unnecessary troubleshooting. Also, as a best practice, ensure that both the fully qualified domain name and IP address endpoints listed in Table 6-2 are reachable. These tables are updated regularly as Microsoft works to build out its network to increase reliability and performance. Subscribing to the RSS feed is recommended in order to get new updates.

Table 6-2. Required IP Addresses, FQDNs, and Ports for Teams Communication

No.	Purpose	Source /Credentials	Destination	ExpressRoute for Office 365 BGP Communities	CIDR Address	Port
1	**Required:** Suite-wide services		See Office 365 required entries for shared services, authentication, and Office Online			
2	**Required:** Microsoft Teams	Client or server / logged-on user	*.teams.skype.com *.teams.microsoft.com teams.microsoft.com	Yes	Microsoft Teams IP ranges	TCP 80 & 443

No.	Purpose	Source ICredentials	Destination	ExpressRoute for Office 365 BGP Communities	CIDR Address	Port
3	**Required:** Microsoft Teams collaboration	Client or server / logged-on user	*.asm.skype.com *.cc.skype.com *.conv.skype.com *.dc.trouter.io *.msg.skype.com prod.registrar.skype.com prod.tpc.skype.com	Yes	Microsoft Teams IP ranges	TCP 443

(continued)

Table 6-2. (*continued*)

No.	Purpose	Source ICredentials	Destination	ExpressRoute for Office 365 BGP Communities	CIDR Address	Port
4	**Required:** Microsoft Teams media	Client or server / logged-on user	These IPs are used by media without explicit FQDN mappings.	Yes	13.107.8.0/24	TCP 443
					13.107.64.0/18	
					52.112.0.0/14	UDP 3478-3481
					104.44.195.0/24	
					104.44.200.0/23	

No.	Purpose	Source /Credentials	Destination	ExpressRoute for Office 365 BGP Communities	CIDR Address	Port
5	**Required:** Microsoft Teams shared services	Client or server / logged-on user	*.config.skype.com *.pipe.skype.com *.pipe.aria.microsoft.com config.edge.skype.com pipe.skype.com s-0001.s-msedge.net s-0004.s-msedge.net scsinstrument-ss-us.trafficmanager.net scsquery-ss-us.trafficmanager.net scsquery-ss-eu.trafficmanager.net scsquery-ss-asia.trafficmanager.net	Yes	Microsoft Teams IP ranges	TCP 443

(continued)

Table 6-2. (*continued*)

No.	Purpose	Source /Credentials	Destination	ExpressRoute for Office 365 BGP Communities	CIDR Address	Port
6	**Required:** Microsoft Teams shared services	Client or server / logged-on user	*.msedge.net compass-ssl.microsoft.com feedback.skype.com	No	N/A	TCP 443
7	**Required:** Microsoft Teams shared services	Client or server / logged-on user	*.secure.skypeassets.com mlccdnprod.azureedge.net videoplayercdn.osi.office.net	No	N/A	TCP 443

No.	Purpose	Source /Credentials	Destination	ExpressRoute for Office 365 BGP Communities	CIDR Address	Port
8	**Optional:** Messaging interop with Skype for Business	Client or server / logged-on user	*.lync.com *.infra.lync.com *.online.lync.com *.resources.lync.com *.skypeforbusiness.com	Yes	Skype for Business IP ranges	TCP 443

(continued)

Table 6-2. (*continued*)

No.	Purpose	Source /Credentials	Destination	ExpressRoute for Office 365 BGP Communities	CIDR Address	Port
9	**Optional:** Messaging interop with Skype for Business (including CDNs)	Client or server / logged-on user	*.azureedge.net *.sfbassets.com latest-swx.cdn.skype.com skypemaprdsitus.trafficmanager.net swx.cdn.skype.com	No	N/A	TCP 443
10	**Optional:** Skype Graph	Client or server / logged-on user	skypegraph.skype.com	No	SkypeGraph. skype.com IP range information	TCP 443

No.	Purpose	Source ICredentials	Destination	ExpressRoute for Office 365 BGP Communities	CIDR Address	Port
11	**Optional:** Yammer third-party integration	Client or server / logged-on user	*.tenor.com	No	N/A	TCP 80 or 443
12	**Optional:** Education features and OneNote integration	Client or server / logged-on user	*.onenote.com	Yes	Office Online IP ranges	TCP 443

(continued)

Port and firewall requirements can be found at `https://support.office.com/en-us/article/office-365-urls-and-ip-address-ranges-8548a211-3fe7-47cb-abb1-355ea5aa88a2?ui=en-US&rs=en-US&ad=US#bkmk_teams_ip`.

In addition, the following is a list of Microsoft Teams services with URLs and their use, make sure these URLs are allowed and accessible.

This simplifies your troubleshooting because Teams services depend on these URLs. If these URLs are not available, finding which URL is not working can take a lot of time and effort.

a. The following URLs are required for Teams sign-in and for organizations that have Active Directory Federation Service servers:

- `https://login.microsoft.com`

- `https://sts.contoso.com`

b. Teams chat and web service are dependent on the following URLs:

- `Teams.microsoft.com`

- `Img.teams.skype.com`

- `Amer-client-ss.msg.skype.com`

- `Emea-client-ss.msg.skype.com`

- `Apac-client-ss.msg.skype.com`

- `*conv.skype.com`

- `*asm.skype.com`

   c. Microsoft Teams calling services depend on the following URLs:

- `*.dc.trouter.io`

- `Prod.tpc.skype.com`

- `Prod.registrar.skype.com`

- `*.cc.skype.com`

   d. The Teams middle tier depends on the following URLs:

- `Api.teams.skype.com`

- `Config.teams.microsoft.com`

   e. Office 365 services including the SharePoint site and OneNote depend on the following URLs:

- `*.sharepoint.com`

- `Onenote.officeapps.live.com`

   f. Services related to Skype for Business Online depend on the following URLs:

- `*.lync.com`

- `*.skypeforbusiness.com`

If you are unable to connect to these URLs, there will be some impact on Teams communication, so make sure to whitelist these URLs.

Remembering all these URLs and IP address is difficult. In addition, Microsoft adds new service URLs or IP addresses, so the recommended way to keep up is to subscribe to RSS feeds. Open Microsoft Teams, select the Store option, and type **RSS**. Once the RSS feeds shows (see Figure 6-17) click it and subscribe.

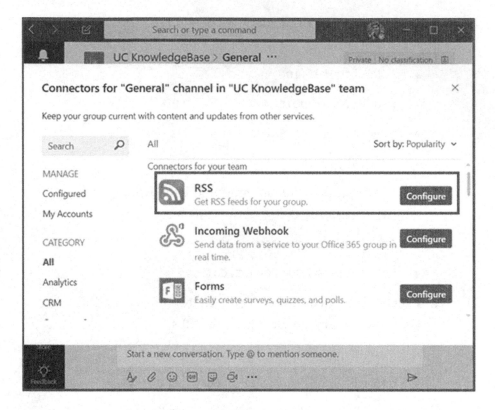

Figure 6-17. *Subscribing to RSS feeds*

Microsoft Teams Common Troubleshooting Scenarios

Microsoft Teams has many capabilities and various workloads, which makes Teams a complex product. Because Teams has multiple features and dependencies on numerous services, the chances of end-user-facing issues increases. For example, users may be unable to connect to the Teams client, Teams groups could have issues, Teams sites could have issues, or calendar information may not be synchronizing.

For example, if a Teams meeting is not showing, that problem will not directly relate to the Teams client, because the Teams client is not directly connecting to the Exchange server. So don't look it directly to Teams client. Basically, the Teams service will autodiscover on behalf of the Teams client and then connect to Exchange Online/Server.

There are different troubleshooting scenarios; for example, Microsoft Teams Administration and enabling teams setting and new features. Microsoft Teams sign-in and authentication issues, Microsoft Teams team and channel management, Microsoft Teams Guest enable and group access etc.

This section covers the most common troubleshooting scenarios.

Microsoft Teams Sign-in and Authentication Troubleshooting

Before focusing on troubleshooting, you need to understand how the Teams sign-in process works

I describe the Teams sign-in process with AD FS in this section, because most organizations use on-premises Active Directory as authoritative for the authority.

So, most of the sign-in process happens in the Office 365 cloud. However, for organization who has on-prem Authentication like, Active Directory Federation Service (AD FS), or organizations can use third-party identity services to authenticate their users. Organizations must keep the AD FS servers or third-party identity servers highly available, because all the clients (including Teams, desktop, mobile, and web clients) are going to use the AD FS or third-party identity servers for authentication. That's why these servers must be available and accessible from all your networks including external, internal, wired/wireless, and VPN.

Here is the sign-in process:

1. The Microsoft Teams client resolves and connects to teams.microsoft.com.

2. The Teams client Adal.login ➤ login.microsoftonline.com

3. Then UserRealm ➤ Federated Domain ADFS URL

4. Then ADFS SAML Token ➤ login.microsoftonline.com

5. An access token and refresh token are issued to the client.

6. After sign-in, the Teams client will retrieve and store the access token (TSAUTHCOOKIE).

Microsoft Teams uses Modern Authentication, which has single sign-on. This has many benefits; for example, being able to sign in to Microsoft Teams without reentering your e-mail and password every time you want to start a new session with Teams. It's a more secure and reliable way to sign in to Microsoft Teams.

Because Microsoft Teams uses Modern Authentication and it's hardcoded, it should be able to recognize your credentials as linked to your Office 365 account. If you are not able to complete the sign-in process, there might be something wrong with your domain or your organization's Office 365 account. Your organization's administrator should Office 365 account to resolve sign-in issues.

Here are the basic troubleshooting steps for sign-in issues:

1. Restart the Microsoft Teams client and log in again.

2. Microsoft Teams uses an Office 365 account. If your computer login account is different from your Office 365 account, sign out and sign in again.

3. Check your network connection and Internet connectivity. Teams is a cloud service, so Internet connectivity is required to connect Teams services.

4. Verify your computer time and date, which will affect connections to secure (HTTPS) web sites.

5. Check and verify that your Active Directory Federation Service or third-party identity service URLs are available and reachable.

If the Active Directory Federation Service (AD FS) server URL is unavailable, the following will display:

`Teams sign-in fails because ADFS URL is unavailable.`

When you capture the Teams desktop client log, it will show a message, as in Figure 6-18:

`Modern Auth failed - failback to web auth`

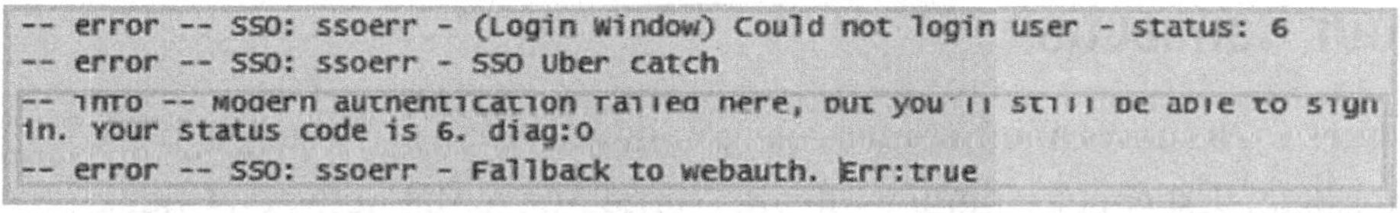

```
-- error -- SSO: ssoerr - (Login window) Could not login user - status: 6
-- error -- SSO: ssoerr - SSO Uber catch
-- info -- Modern authentication failed here, but you'll still be able to sign
in. Your status code is 6. diag:0
-- error -- SSO: ssoerr - Fallback to webauth. Err:true
```

Figure 6-18. *ADFS service unavailable*

D'oh! Something Went Wrong

When authentication fails with "D'oh!" restart your client. If that doesn't work, try signing out and signing back in (see Figure 6-19).

Figure 6-19. *Restart the client after login failure*

Oh No ... We Can't Connect to the Internet—Check your Connection

Figure 6-20 shows another message you might receive. If you see this message, first check whether you are connected to the network. Check your wired or wireless connectivity and then click the Restart button to start the Teams client again.

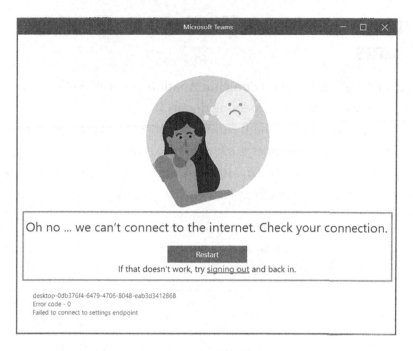

Figure 6-20. *Teams client unable to connect*

If that doesn't help, click the Signing Out link and then sign back in.

Microsoft Teams Internal Client Failed to Sign In

If form-based authentication is not enabled in your AD FS server for the intranet, you will see errors because forms-based authentication is required for Teams to sign in internally. All Internet or external clients will use Windows authentication by default.

In the preceding case, all external clients will be signed in; however, all internal clients will fail because forms-based authentication is not available.

Unable to See Teams Meeting / No Meeting in Teams

If the user is unable to see meeting information, the user will see the error, "Sorry. We couldn't get your meeting details."

If the Microsoft Teams client cannot connect to `api.teams.skype.com`, there can be a different reason, such as an organization block (see Figure 6-21). Teams meeting join issue may be service connectivity problem or network connectivity issue which you may notice in your environment.

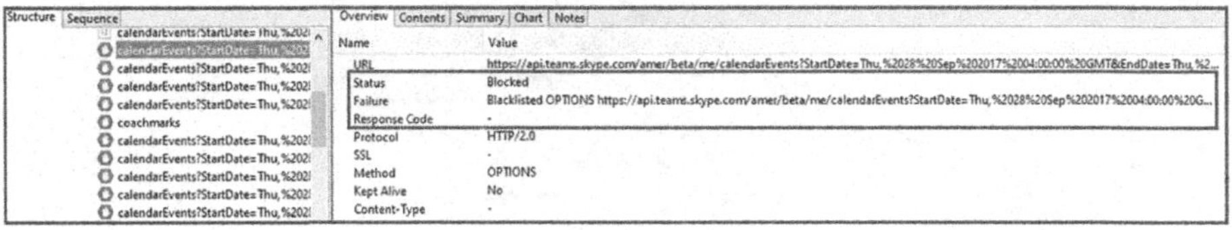

Figure 6-21. *Service URL blocked*

Make sure `api.teams.skype.com` is not blocked; otherwise, the calendar event will not show up.

Troubleshooting Guest Access in Microsoft Teams

You can allow and disallow Microsoft Teams guest access in multiple places. This allows your organization to granularly control Teams guest access by using different levels.

- *Azure Active Directory*: In Azure Active Directory, you can allow or disallow guest access and control at the AAD level.

- *Office 365 Groups*: You can also control guest access at the Office 365 group level.

- *SharePoint and OneDrive for Business*: You can control access for SharePoint and OneDrive for Business.

- *Microsoft Teams*: Teams has its own control for guest access on a per teams basis.

For example, If you enable guest access in Microsoft Teams, you can set rules to allow guest access in SharePoint. If you disable guest access (external access) in Azure Active Directory, guest access will not work in Teams or SharePoint.

Enable Guest Access in Azure Active Directory

To enable guest access in Azure Active Directory, log in to the Office 365 Admin portal. Open the Azure Active Directory Admin Center, and click Azure Active Directory ➤ Users ➤ User Settings. In User Settings, the External Access section shows four options:

- Guest users permissions are limited

- Admins and users in the guest inviter role can invite

- Members can invite

- Guest can invite

To allow or disallow access, simply toggle on or off the appropriate option. Figure 6-22 shows the ideal allowed access for guests.

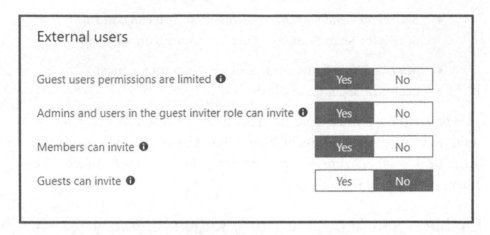

Figure 6-22. *Guest access settings*

Enable Guest Access in Office 365 Groups

After enabling guest access in Azure Active Directory, it's time to enable guest access in Office 365 groups. Here are the steps:

Log in to the Office 365 Admin portal. Select Settings and then Services and Add-ins. Find the Office 365 Groups option and open it. Here, you can control settings for Office 365 groups.

Toggle on the appropriate setting, as shown in Figure 6-23:

- Let group members outside the organization access group content

- Let group owners add people outside the organization to group

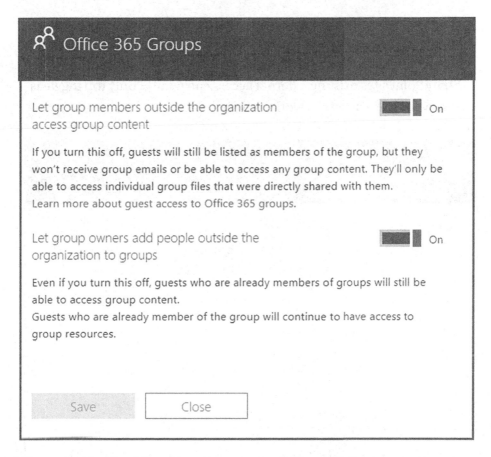

Figure 6-23. *Enabling guest access via Office 365 Groups*

Enable Guest in SharePoint and OneDrive for Business

In SharePoint also, you can allow or disable guest/external access for users. Here are the steps:

Log in to the Office 365 Admin portal. Expand Settings and select Services and Add-ins. Find Sites and open it. In Sites, you can update your sites settings.

Allow external sharing by setting the toggle on for "Let users share SharePoint Online and OneDrive for Business content with people outside the organization," as shown in Figure 6-24.

SharePoint sites existing external access can control only top toggle is necessary for guest access to work with files.

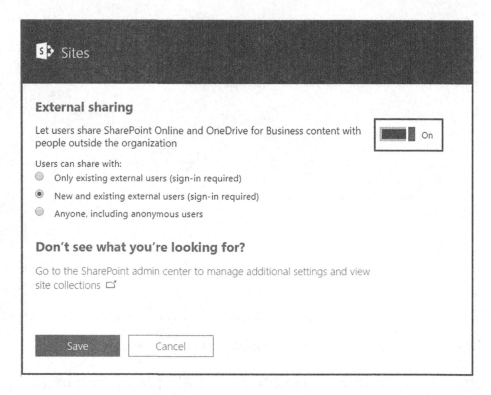

Figure 6-24. Guest access in SharePoint and OneDrive for Business

Enable Guest Access in Microsoft Teams Itself

As of March 2018, there is only one place for enabling guest access in Teams that will be a complete tenant-wide setting (applicable to the whole tenant). You select Guest under Settings by User/License Type, as shown in Figure 6-25.

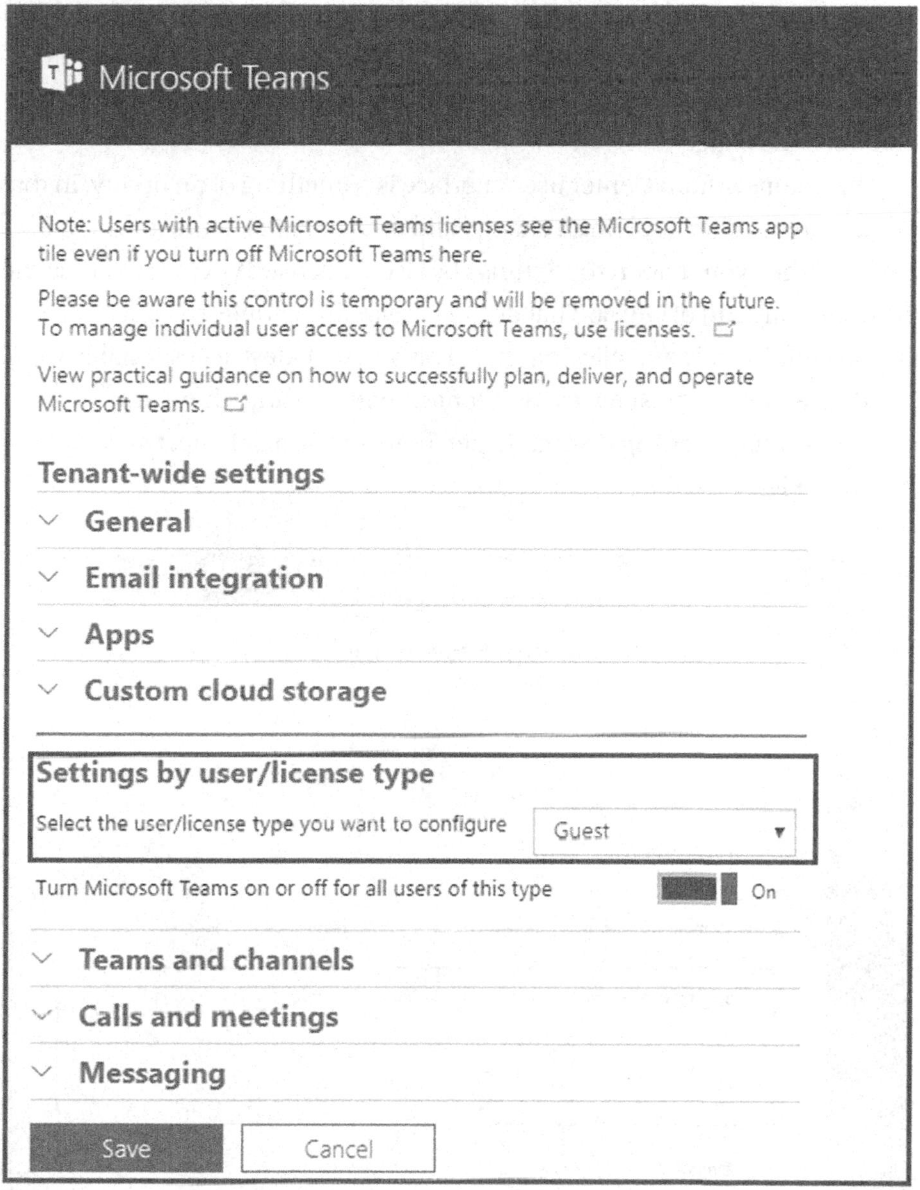

Microsoft Teams

Note: Users with active Microsoft Teams licenses see the Microsoft Teams app tile even if you turn off Microsoft Teams here.

Please be aware this control is temporary and will be removed in the future. To manage individual user access to Microsoft Teams, use licenses. ⊡

View practical guidance on how to successfully plan, deliver, and operate Microsoft Teams. ⊡

Tenant-wide settings

∨ **General**

∨ **Email integration**

∨ **Apps**

∨ **Custom cloud storage**

Settings by user/license type

Select the user/license type you want to configure | Guest ▼ |

Turn Microsoft Teams on or off for all users of this type   ▮▮ On

∨ **Teams and channels**

∨ **Calls and meetings**

∨ **Messaging**

| Save | Cancel |

Figure 6-25. *Enabling guest access in Microsoft Teams*

Log in to the Office 365 Admin portal. Expand Settings and select Services and Add-ins. Find the Microsoft Teams option and open it. In Microsoft Teams, select Guest under Settings by User/License type and then Save the page.

The Teams Admin Center user interface is something of an oddity, in that it kicks you out after applying a change and then defaults to the first item in that list. When you reopen the Settings by User/License Type, you will see the first option instead of Guest. That doesn't mean the settings did not apply; after selecting Guest and clicking Save. This will do Guest access enable work.

After enabling guest access as a tenant-wide setting, there are additional Teams settings available per Teams to control guest access, as shown in Figure 6-26.

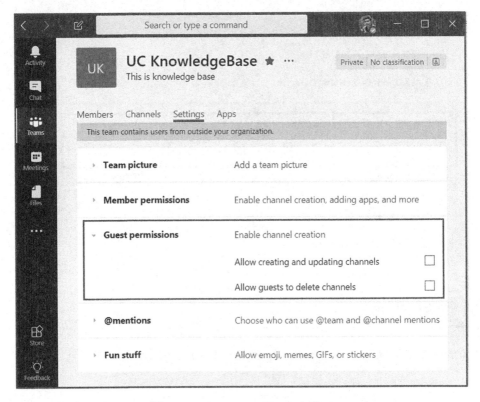

Figure 6-26. *Controlling guest access permissions*

Guest access permission and control for specific Teams, to do this uncheck below option:

- Allow creating and updating channels

- Allow guests to delete channels

Once you allow guest access and adding new guests to your teams, you can send a guest access invitation (send token) to a guest e-mail address. After the guest clicks Open Microsoft Teams, the invite gets accepted. Then the access token gets accepted. You can see the activity as "Redeem external user invite" success in Azure Active Directory.

If there is an issue with the access token, you can check the activity log or auditing log in the Azure Active Directory Admin Center.

If you added a guest to your team but that guest is not seeing an invitation, check the audit logs in the Azure Active Directory Admin Center, as shown in Figure 6-27. Find the Initiated By field to see whether the Add User activity successfully happened.

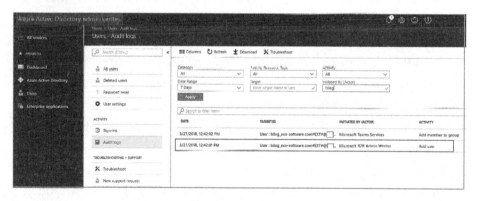

Figure 6-27. *Audit logs for guest access*

Best Practices

When trobuleshootinging guest access issues, a top-to-bottom approch is important. There are many moving pieces, so make sure guest access is properly enabled and then look at the auditing logs and do more analysis.

If issues persist, open tickets with Microsoft and share log details with Microsoft Support Team.

One-to-One Audio/Video Calling Issue in Microsoft Teams

As you know, Microsoft Teams has multiple features, including chat, collaboration, audio/video calls, meetings, and PSTN calls. Audio/video calls involve two workloads: signaling and media.

In Microsoft Teams, signaling always uses TCP/port 443, and media uses UDP 50,000 to 50,059 for direct media connections (audio port range: 50,000–50,019, video port range: 50,020–50,039, and application and desktop sharing: 50,040–50,059)

If two clients will be directly talking to each other over a high port range but there is a firewall between the two clients and direct connectivity is not possible, these two clients will talk to each other via transport relay using UDP port 3478–3481 or TCP port 443.

By default, ICE will try to negotiate over UDP port 3478–3481, and if that doesn't work, will fall back to TCP over port 443.

If there is an issue in audio/video calls, something between the two clients might be blocking communication. Here are the most common causes:

- Security application may intervene

- Multiple virtual adaptors or virtual machines

- Network device blocking connection

The following are best practices for troubleshooting audio/video calls:

- Allow all required IP addresses, fully qualified domain names, and port ranges from your corporate firewall to the Office 365 cloud.

- If Teams audio/video calls always fail, try to isolate the affected computer by using a different computer with the Teams client and then test audio/video calls.

- If you are using any USB device (speaker and mic), disconnect the device and then make the audio/video call and validate calls again.

- Capture Teams call network traffic by using Wireshark or NetMon and see whether any media packets are getting dropped.

Microsoft Teams Meeting Join Failed

As I mentioned earlier, every Teams call or meeting has two types of traffic: signaling and media.

If a meeting join fails, Teams will give the exact cause of for the failure via an error message such as this:

> *It looks like your network configuration is preventing us from making your call. Please contact your network admin for help and don't forget to show them what's behind that More Information button.*

This error message clearly mentions that there is a network issue preventing the meeting join. When I looked over the web log showing that the call terminated, the reason was call setup failure:

```
CallstatusChanged: Terminated, reason = 7, Call Setup Failure.
```

In this case, something prevented the call setup. Most issues related to TCP connectivity are caused by a firewall. Make sure to check that all required URLs, IP addresses, and ports are opened in the firewall or proxy. Refer to Table 6-2 for a list of IPs, FQDNs, and port requirements.

In Microsoft Teams, the client will use TCP/443 port signaling and UDP 3478 to 3481 for media. If UDP ports are not available, media will fall back to TURN relay over TCP/443.

Tips and Tricks for Microsoft Teams

Microsoft Teams has many capabilities, so using the tips and tricks presented in this section will enhance your Teams usage.

Schedule a Teams Meeting by Using Outlook Calendar

You can schedule a Teams meeting by using your Outlook calendar.

Open Outlook. Then click New Items ➤ Teams Meeting, as shown in Figure 6-28.

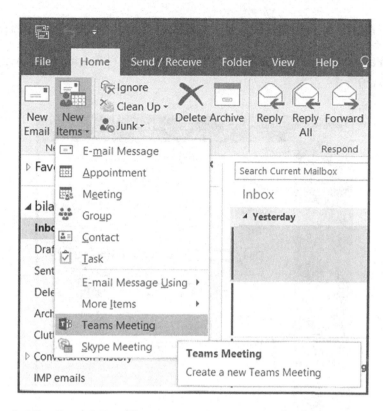

Figure 6-28. *Creating a Teams meeting via Outlook*

Schedule a Meeting by Using the Teams Client

You can also schedule a meeting by using Microsoft Teams, as shown in Figure 6-29.

Figure 6-29. *Scheduling meetings in Microsoft Teams*

Tag People to Get Your Message Noticed

You can use @mentions to call attention to your message.

In the team conversation, start typing your message (see Figure 6-30).

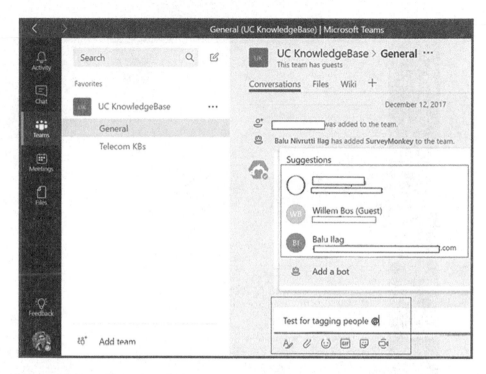

Figure 6-30. *Tag people in your message*

Type @, followed by your teammate's name or e-mail address, and select Teammate who user search.

That person will get a notification in their inbox and activity feed about the conversation.

Tag your Teams as Favorite Teams

Tag your favorite teams, and they'll appear at the top of your Favorites list for quick and easy access (see Figure 6-31).

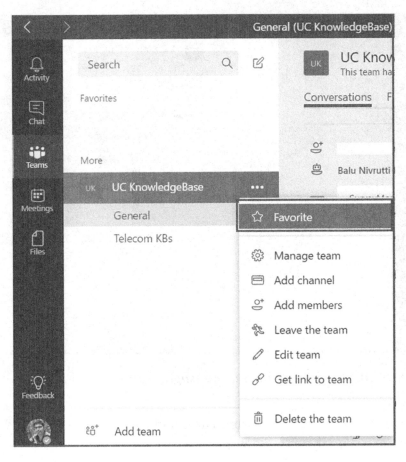

Figure 6-31. *Adding a team as a favorite*

In your Teams list, find one of the teams or channels you work with most often.

Click the More icon to the right of the name and then select Favorite.

Speed Up your Teams Use by Using Keyboard Shortcuts

For people who have difficulty using the mouse, keyboard shortcuts provide a great alternative.

In the Teams app, press Alt+/ to display a list of available keyboard shortcuts (see Figure 6-32).

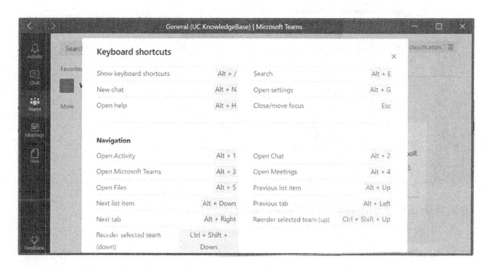

Figure 6-32. *Teams keyboard shortcuts*

Complete Keyboard Shortcuts List   You can read this blog article for complete list of shortcuts: `http://communicationsknowledge.blogspot.in/#!/2017/12/expedite-your-microsoft-teams-uses.html`

Make Collaborating on Files a Breeze

Ready for some team bonding? Coauthoring with your team has never been easier.

On the menu at the top of your channel (above the conversations), click Files. Click New to create a new file, or Upload to upload an existing one (see Figure 6-33).

Figure 6-33. *Uploading a file in the channel*

Now all your teammates can open the file in the browser, or in the desktop app, to write and edit collaboratively.

It's All About Meme

You can also add GIFs to inject some personality into your conversations.

To add a GIF to your reply, just click at the bottom of your conversation view. Search for, or select, a GIF from the picker (see Figure 6-34). Click Send when you're ready.

Figure 6-34. *Adding meme images*

Next, type anything—for example, **happy**.

Then select any GIF (Figure 6-35).

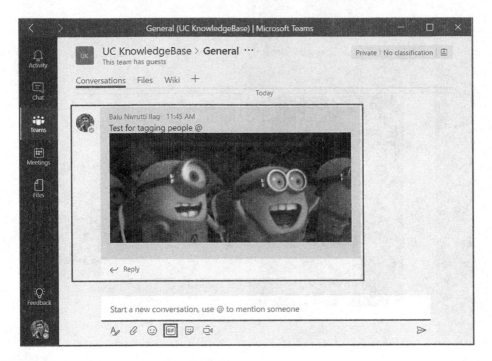

Figure 6-35. *Adding a GIF*

For more information, watch "More Productive Conversations with Microsoft Teams" on YouTube (`www.youtube.com/watch?v=zQOFCOSMOwY`).

Ask Teams-Related Questions to T-Bot

T-Bot is always available to answer all Teams-related queries. If you have a question about Microsoft Teams, T-Bot is here to help!

Go to the Chat list and you'll find T-Bot listed in the user panel at the left. Click it and type your question in the chat panel. T-Bot will get right back to you with an answer, as shown in Figure 6-36.

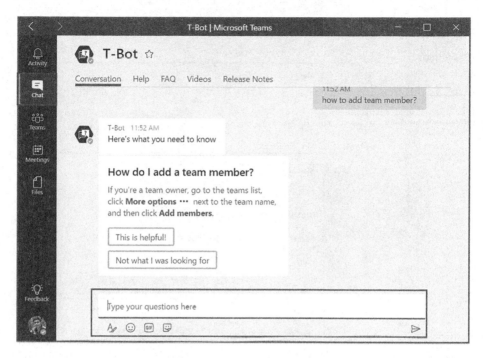

Figure 6-36. *Teams T-Bot*

T-Bot is available in English, French, German, and Spanish!

If you want to create your own, custom, bot for Microsoft Teams, refer to https://msdn.microsoft.com/en-us/microsoft-teams/bots.

Always Be in the Know with Notifications

Notifications keep you current with what's happening in your Teams. Turn them on, turn them off, choose how and when to be notified: it's all up to you.

1. Click your picture at the bottom-left corner.

2. Choose Settings ➤ Notifications (see Figure 6-37).

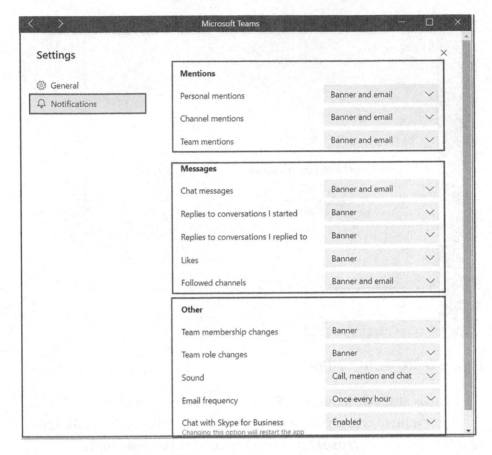

Figure 6-37. *Teams notifications*

    3.   For each type of notification, choose an option.

These options help you keep track of conversations, messages, mentions, and team membership changes.

Use Microsoft Teams on Mobile to Be More Responsive

The Teams mobile app is available on iOS, Android, and Windows Phone. Using the Teams mobile app, you can participate in conversations, connecting and collaborating wherever you are.

Using Teams mobile apps, you can see all of your teams, channels, files, and more.

Simply click your photo in Teams and then click Download the Mobile App. Type your e-mail address to send the Teams mobile app URL so you can download mobile apps (Figure 6-38).

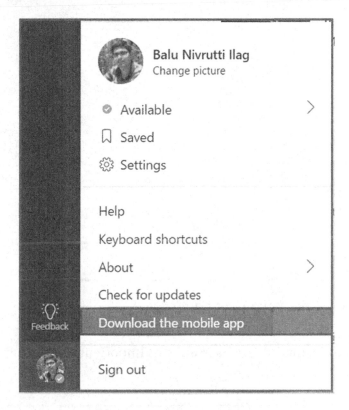

Figure 6-38. *Downloading the Teams mobile app*

Marking Chats as Important Can Help Your Topic Stand Out

Adding *Important* in chats or conversations helps members understand the significance of a topic. Marking a conversation as Important is easy. Click the button to expand the compose box (it looks like an A with a pen).

Then type your message and press Enter to post your new conversation (see Figure 6-39).

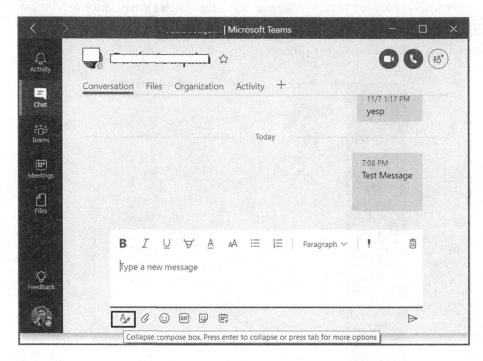

Figure 6-39. *Creating a Teams message*

Now you can mark this conversation as Important, as shown in Figure 6-40.

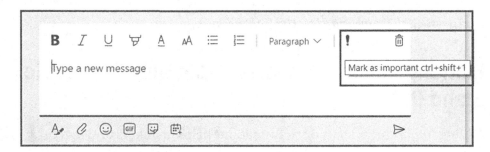

Figure 6-40. *Marking the message as important*

You can learn more about having productive conversations at `https://support.office.com/en-US/article/Productive-conversations-99d33aaa-0743-47c6-a476-eb0a24abcb7e?wt.mc_id=otc_tips`.

Connect Your Team with Connectors

Did you know you can set up a Twitter feed for your team? And you can connect many other services too, including Trello, GitHub, Bing News, and more. With Office 365 connectors, it's easy to connect many of your favorite apps and services. Here's how:

1. Right-click the channel you want to add a connector to.

2. Select Connectors.

3. Search for the connector(s) you want to add to the channel.

4. Click Add and follow the prompts.

To learn more about connecting your Teams, see `https://msdn.microsoft.com/en-us/microsoft-teams/connectors`.

Stay in the Loop with Activity Alerts

The Activity tab notifies you when somebody @mentions you, likes something you posted, or replies to a thread you started. The number on the Activity bell indicates how many alerts you have waiting.

You'll find the Activity tab at the top of the navigation pane on the left. What's on your activity feed?

`https://support.office.com/en-US/article/Whats-on-your-activity-feed-afe6d0c5-34f3-4469-b7bd-905aab4042a3?wt.mc_id=otc_tips`

Teams Monitoring, Reporting, and Analytics

Teams has many capabilities that depend on cloud services, so monitoring these services and checking Teams usage is another important task.

Microsoft Teams Service Health Checks

The Office 365 Admin Center portal is the right place to check Office 365 cloud service health status to verify whether Teams services are healthy.

Microsoft Teams has multiple features, so it has dependencies on other services such as Exchange, SharePoint, and OneDrive for Business. Service health issues for these other services does not automatically mean that Teams is impacted; however, some functionalities may not work correctly.

It's recommended to frequently visit the Office 365 Admin Center and check service health. To check service health, log in to the Office 356 portal with Administrator permission and then click Admins to Office 365 Admin center then Home page click on Service Health to open service health for all Office Services.

There are three status options, indicating by different symbols (see Figure 6-41):

- *Service is healthy*: This will display the service state for all services in summary view.

- *Advisory*: Indicates services that currently have an advisory posted

- *Incident*: Indicates services currently experiencing an incident

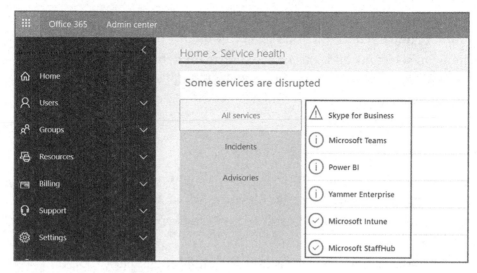

Figure 6-41. *Microsoft Teams Service Health*

Call Quality Dashboard

Achieving good call quality is important for any real-time communication product. Displaying the existing call-quality trends can help you achieve the desired call quality.

Microsoft Teams has a Call Quality Dashboard (CQD) that is available for both Microsoft Teams and Skype for Business Online. Under the Call Quality Dashboard, there is a filter for Microsoft Teams and Skype for Business Online.

The CQD provides insight about the quality of calls made by using Microsoft Teams and Skype for Business services. The dashboard is designed to help Skype for Business and Microsoft Teams admins and network engineers optimize the network. Both Microsoft Teams and Skype for Business traffic travel over your organization's network, so any changes made to the network to improve the audio experience will also directly translate to improvements in video and desktop sharing. So, improving your existing network is key—for example, sizing the wireless access point correctly, adding extra bandwidth if there are bandwidth constraints, minimizing the VPN usage or implementing a VPN split tunnel, implementing Quality of Service, or refreshing old network hardware or appliances.

The CQD plays an important role in showing all call-quality data in summary and detail views. You see all call-quality data aggregated together when you select All, and you see separate team data by selecting the Teams filter. Seeing your users' call quality will be helpful when you are piloting Teams or moving to Teams.

Opening CQD

To open the CQD, log in to the Office 365 Admin Center. Expand the Admin Center and click Skype for Business Admin Center. Remember, the CQD is common to both Microsoft Teams and Skype for Business Online with filter options.

When the Skype for Business Admin Center opens, click Tools and then select Skype for Business Online Call Quality Dashboard to open the CQD (see Figure 6-42).

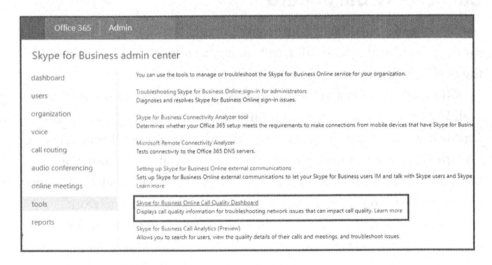

Figure 6-42. *Skype for Business CQD option*

You can also browse to `https://cqd.lync.com` to open the Call Quality Dashboard.

Reading the Report

After you log in to the CQD, you will see the Summary Reports option. If you want to see a detailed report, click Summary Reports and select Detailed Report, as shown in Figure 6-43.

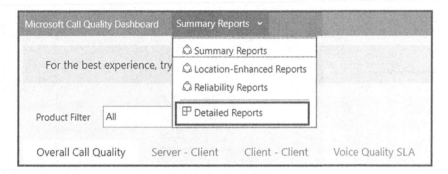

Figure 6-43. *Opening CQD details reports*

Viewing Teams-Specific Call Quality Dashboard

As I mentioned earlier, you can select the Product Filter drop-down menu from the top of the CQD screen and select Microsoft Teams. As soon as the filter applies, you will see summary reports for call quality (see Figure 6-44).

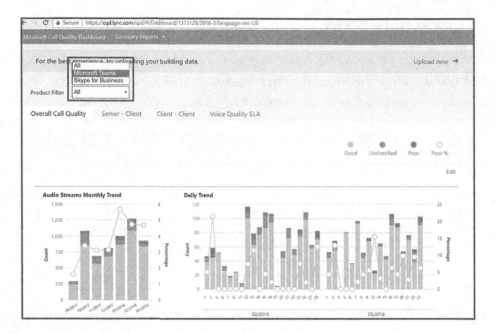

Figure 6-44. *Call Quality Dashboard for Teams*

These summary reports show call-quality graphs and trends. You'll see four options for viewing call-quality trends, as shown in Figure 6-45:

- Overall Call Quality

- Server – Client

- Client – Client

- Voice Quality SLA

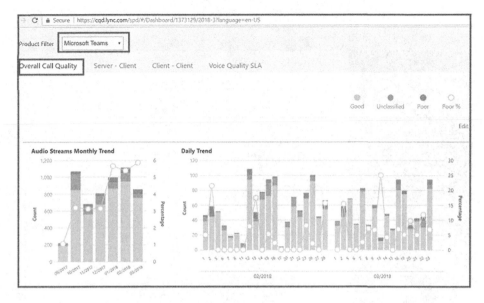

Figure 6-45. *CQD Overall Call Quality*

Audit Logs for Microsoft Teams Events

Audit logs are important because they track each activity, who makes changes that break service, and users' experiences. If a user deletes a document in Teams, or if a Teams administrator adds a guest user to Teams, logs record this information.

You can search the Office 365 audit log to find out what the users and administrators in your organization have been doing. You, as an Office 365 administrator, will be able to find activity related to e-mail, groups, documents, permissions, directory services, and much more.

Figure 6-46 shows the Microsoft Teams list of activities that can be audited.

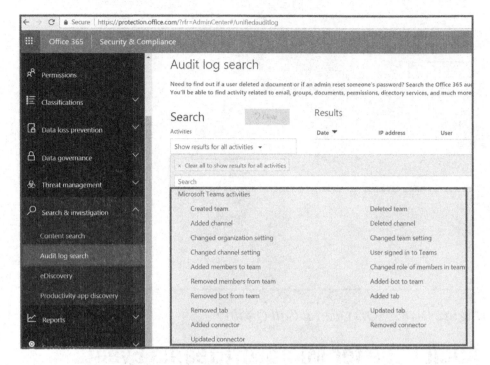

Figure 6-46. *Audit log search*

Figure 6-47 shows the Microsoft Teams activities.

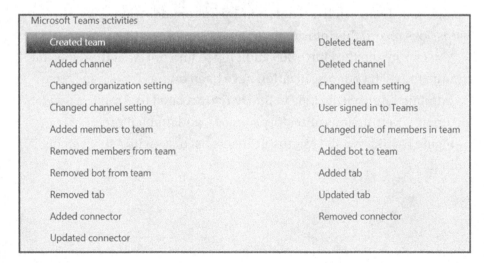

Figure 6-47. *Audit activity list*

For critical workload auditing, you can set up e-mail alerts as well. Those e-mail alerts can go to your favorite Teams channel.

Future Problem Solving: Microsoft Teams and Skype for Business Admin Center Tool

Microsoft will soon present the Microsoft Teams & Skype for Business Admin Center with all kinds of administrator settings and analytics. Although it's not a troubleshooting solution today, its preview view with the following limited options is available now (see Figure 6-48):

- Call Analytics (Preview)

- User Search

- Sites

- Settings: Permission

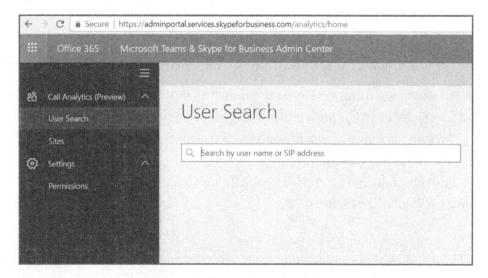

Figure 6-48. *Microsoft Teams & Skype for Business Admin Center (Preview)*

Microsoft will be adding new capabilities to the Microsoft Teams & Skype for Business Admin Center. Some of these capabilities include the following:

- *Microsoft Teams messaging policy*: Create a policy for user-level management of the Microsoft Teams client experience for messaging scenarios.

- *Microsoft Teams interop policy*: Configure the interoperability experience between Skype for Business and Microsoft Teams.

- *Microsoft Teams guest messaging settings*: Control the messaging capabilities for guest accounts in Microsoft Teams.

- *Federation settings*: Manage the federation between tenants for Microsoft Teams and Skype for Business.

- *User management*: Assign policies and configure user accounts.

- *Audio conferencing*: Configure dial-in numbers and settings for Skype for Business and Microsoft Teams.

All existing settings for General, Email Integration, Custom Cloud Storage, Calls and Meetings, and Messaging in Microsoft Teams will be migrated to the new Microsoft Teams & Skype for Business Admin Center over the next few months.

The new, fully functional Microsoft Teams & Skype for Business Admin Center will look like Figure 6-49.

Figure 6-49. *Future look of Microsoft Teams and Skype for Business Admin Center*

Table 6-3 shows the Microsoft Teams admin-level settings that are going to be available in the new admin center, this current Teams experience that will be migrated and shows the relationship between the current settings and the policies in the new admin center.

Table 6-3. *Teams and Skype for Business Admin Center Policy availability setting:*

SECTION OF TEAMS IN OFFICE 365 ADMIN CENTER	SETTING NAME (TENANT LEVEL)	MICROSOFT TEAMS & SKYPE FOR BUSINESS ADMIN CENTER POLICY	LEVEL: TENANT OR USER
General	Show organizational chat in personal profile	TeamsClientConfiguration	Tenant
General	Use Skype for Business for recipients who don't have Teams	TeamsClientConfiguration	Tenant
General	Allow T-Bot proactive help messages	TeamsClientConfiguration	Tenant
Email integration	Allow users to send emails to channels	TeamsClientConfiguration	Tenant
Email integration	Allow senders list	TeamsClientConfiguration	Tenant
Custom cloud storage	Box	TeamsClientConfiguration	Tenant
Custom cloud storage	Dropbox	TeamsClientConfiguration	Tenant
Custom cloud storage	Google Drive	TeamsClientConfiguration	Tenant

(continued)

Table 6-3. (*continued*)

SECTION OF TEAMS IN OFFICE 365 ADMIN CENTER	SETTING NAME (TENANT LEVEL)	MICROSOFT TEAMS & SKYPE FOR BUSINESS ADMIN CENTER POLICY	LEVEL: TENANT OR USER
Custom cloud storage	ShareFile	TeamsClientConfiguration	Tenant
Settings by user/license type	Turn Microsoft Teams on or off for all users	Deprecated. Use Office 365 admin center to assign licenses.	
Teams and channels		Redirects to AAD Group Management (Same as current experience).	User
Calls and meetings	Allow scheduling for private meetings	TeamsMeetingPolicy	User
Calls and meetings	Allow ad hoc channel meetup	TeamsMeetingPolicy	User
Calls and meetings	Allow scheduling for channel meetings	TeamsMeetingPolicy	User
Calls and meetings	Allow videos in meetings	TeamsMeetingPolicy	User
Calls and meetings	Allow screen sharing in meetings	TeamsMeetingPolicy	User
Calls and meetings	Allow private calling	TeamsCallingPolicy	User

(*continued*)

Table 6-3. (*continued*)

SECTION OF TEAMS IN OFFICE 365 ADMIN CENTER	SETTING NAME (TENANT LEVEL)	MICROSOFT TEAMS & SKYPE FOR BUSINESS ADMIN CENTER POLICY	LEVEL: TENANT OR USER
Messaging	Enable Giphy so users can add gifs to conversations	TeamsMessagingPolicy	User
Messaging	Content rating	TeamsMessagingPolicy	User
Messaging	Enable memes that users can edit and add to conversations	TeamsMessagingPolicy	User
Messaging	Enable stickers that users can edit and add to conversations	TeamsMessagingPolicy	User
Messaging	Allow owners to delete all messages	TeamsMessagingPolicy	User
Messaging	Allow users to edit their own messages	TeamsMessagingPolicy	User
Messaging	Allow users to delete their own messages	TeamsMessagingPolicy	User
Messaging	Allows users to chat privately	TeamsMessagingPolicy	User

Summary

This chapter focused exclusively on Teams client- and service-side troubleshooting. Microsoft Teams has many features, and these capabilities have dependencies that make Teams unique as well as complex. Before spending time on investigation of issues, check the service health. Service health for Microsoft Teams is displayed on the Office 365 Admin portal main page. Before troubleshooting issues with the client, it is good practice to verify that the Teams service is healthy and to look for any service degradation alerts.

The next step in troubleshooting is to gather the client logs; without a diagnostic log, you cannot do any in-depth troubleshooting. That's why an important part of troubleshooting is capturing the right diagnostic logs. Microsoft Teams has a client for each platform (including Windows, macOS, iOS, Android, and web client), and these clients have rich logging capabilities that will assist in troubleshooting many end-user problems. Because each client log-capturing method is different, this chapter shows how to gather diagnostic logs for each client. After capturing a log, you can use any text editor to analyze the it.

This chapter covers most common troubleshooting scenarios. Microsoft Teams has many capabilities and numerous workloads, which makes Teams a complex product. Because Teams has multiple features as well as dependencies on various, the chances of end-user-facing issues increase (for example, users being unable to connect to a Teams client, or calendar information not synchronizing). Microsoft Teams has different workloads, so analyzing call quality is another important step. To analyze the call quality, you can use the Call Quality Dashboard that is available for Microsoft Teams and Skype for Business Online. You can see all call-quality data aggregated together or as separate teams data. This will helpful when you are piloting Teams or moving to Teams, so you can see the call quality for your users. Finally, audit logs are important for tracking activities, Teams has a huge list of activities that are logged, and you can search these activity logs for auditing purposes.

Glossary

AAD: Azure Active Directory

AD: Active Directory

ADAL: Azure Active Directory Authentication Library

Candidate: Possible combination of IP address and port for media channel

CDR: Call Detail Record

CQD: Call Quality Dashboard

DID: direct inward dialing

DSCP: Differentiated Service Code Point

EWS: Exchange Web Services

ExpressRoute: An Azure service that lets you create private connections between Microsoft datacenters and infrastructure that's on your premises or in a colocation facility.

FQDN: fully qualified domain name

GPO: Group Policy Object

HTTPS: Hypertext Transfer Protocol Secure

ICE: Interactive Connectivity Establishment

InterOp: interoperability

ITSP: Internet telephony service provider

LAN: local area network

MDM: mobile device management

NAT: network address translation

OS: operating system

PBX: private branch exchange

PLC: professional learning community

© Balu N Ilag 2018
B.N. Ilag, *Introducing Microsoft Teams*, https://doi.org/10.1007/978-1-4842-3567-6

PRI line: A Primary Rate Interface (PRI) line is a form of Integrated Services Digital Network (ISDN) line, which is a telecommunication standard that enables traditional phone lines to carry voice, data, and video traffic, among others.

PSOM: Persistent Shared Object Model protocol

PSTN: public switched telephone network

QoE: Quality of Experience

QoS: Quality of Service

Relay: media relay or transport relay

REST API: Representational State Transfer application programming interface

RTP: Real-Time Transport Protocol

SBC: session border controller

SCCM: System Center Configuration Manager

SCOM: System Center Operations Manager

SIP: Session Initiation Protocol

SIP trunk: SIP trunking is a Voice over Internet Protocol (VoIP) technology and streaming media service based on the Session Initiation Protocol (SIP) by which Internet telephony service providers (ITSPs) deliver telephone services.

SSO: single sign-on

STUN: Simple Traversal of UDP through NAT / Session Traversal Utilities for NAT

TCP: Transport Control Protocol

TRAP: Transport Relay Authentication Provider

TURN: Traversal Using Relay NAT

UDP: User Datagram Protocol

URI: Uniform Resource Identifier

URL: Uniform Resource Locator

WAN: wide area network

Index

CPSIA information can be obtained
at www.ICGtesting.com
Printed in the USA
LVOW13s0912050718
582769LV00008B/206/P

9 781484 235669